Power of Positivity
for Bipolar and Anyone Else

Learning to develop the power of positivity in my life, I encountered many challenges while dealing with bipolar disorder. This book explores these challenges and how I ultimately achieved episode-free stability. In the Power of Positivity, I present the numerous sources that were an inspiration to me and led me to a positive state of mind. After more than fifty years of struggling with bipolar disorder, I have written this book to help others achieve long-term stability.

Power of Positivity
for Bipolar and Anyone Else

Fred L. Von Gunten, O.D.

Follow Dr. Fred on:
Blog Spot
Twitter
Facebook
Daily Strength (must be a member)

Available as an eBook at

-Smashwords: www.smashwords.com
-Amazon Kindle: www.amazon.com
-Barnes & Noble:
www.barnesandnoble.com
-Diesel: www.diesel-ebooks.com
-Kobo: www.kobobooks.com
-Apple iTunes: www.apple.com/iTunes
Cover Image Copyright 2011 Tony
Johnson
ISBN-13: 978-1478110149
ISBN-10: 1478110147

Acknowledgements

My profound thanks to my wife Linda, who without her love and true devotion and constant support, I could never have achieved control and my long stability with bipolar disorder.

In addition, sincere thanks to my dear friend and editor, Linda Lee Rathbun, (www.naturalwanders.com), who without her dedication and knowledge, this book could not have been completed. Also, I want to thank Tony Johnson for his outstanding cover design; Tony's awesome artwork can be seen on Facebook, www.facebook.com/thatsjustthewayitis (log in, then navigate to Tony's Photos).

This book could not have been written without the generous assistance of countless individuals who struggle with bipolar disorder and who shared their experiences and knowledge. To all my friends and family who supported me, I extend my deep appreciation.

Forward by Linda Von Gunten

At a certain stage in my marriage, I decided that I was not going to ride on the bipolar roller coaster the rest of my life. Around that time, my therapist asked if I was going to divorce Fred because of his bipolar moods. Ironically, bipolar disorder prompted positivity in our lives.

As Fred and I came to a crossroad with how to live with bipolar disorder, rather than separate our family, I thought about Fred's abundant qualities. These were the reasons I married him, and they were all positive reasons for staying in the marriage.

Because of a past genetic history of bipolar disorder in Fred's family, his mother found it impossible to accept the disorder and stayed in denial. It was then that our professional advisors suggested that we sever all ties with her and members of that side of the family. It took about ten years for us to become a healthy nuclear family unit. It was then that both Fred and I found better communication skills and could ease our way back into a caring, loving and accepting extended family.

Our professional support system guided us to an understanding of our individual qualities and helped us come together as a stronger, self-confident couple. I found that some changes needed to be made. I was a passive doormat; Fred was an aggressive control person as a result of his bipolar moods. I needed to become more assertive and Fred needed to be less controlling and to understand when episodes were imminent. With professional help, we accomplished this.

In order to go forward in my life, I had to challenge some difficult issues in my past to overcome the causes of my passive personality. I became more confident and these new feelings helped me cope with living with a bipolar person. This helped Fred to better understand my personal needs. As Fred learned more about himself, we could help each other to find new and positive goals.

As our children grew, they gained knowledge about bipolar disorder from Fred and I, and by researching information on the subject on their own. It was this awareness, and hard work that made us a positive family unit, and that made living with bipolar disorder easier.

Table of Contents

Acknowledgements

Forward by Linda Von Gunten

Chapter 1:

My Life with Bipolar Disorder

"Look not mournfully into the past. It comes not back again. Wisely improve the present. It is thine. Go forth to meet the shadowy future, without fear." Henry Wadsworth Longfellow.

I believe in the "power of positivity." This book will work toward proving the benefits of positivity over negativity.

My name is Dr. Fred and I have been retired for over 13 years. I was an Optometrist, specializing in developmental and behavioral vision for more than 33 years. I gave sight to others to learn from their insight. I am happily married to a lovely lady, 48 years and counting. She supported me during my episodes and I owe my life to her. At age 70, I have knowledge and experience when it comes to dealing with bipolar disorder. Therefore, my mission is to help others in achieving emotional stability without episodes. I have lived 50 years with bipolar I. For the first 25 years, I dealt with over five episodes. Since then, I have transformed my life by changing my thoughts and committing to a consistent supply of Lithium. I have maintained years of "episode-free emotional stability." Some would classify this as a "functional bipolar". Perhaps I might classify it as "functionally cured." I was one of the first to receive Lithium when the FDA approved it in 1971. It has kept me stable for the last 28 years, along with knowing the "Power of Being Positive with Bipolar Disorder."

Question...Have you considered the long-term effects of the Lithium on your thyroid and kidneys? Over 40 years of taking Lithium is a long time. When creatinine levels in your kidneys are beginning to rise and your therapeutic level with Lithium is no longer 0.7, but is creeping toward toxic levels of 1.4 to 1.9, will your success with stability come tumbling down as a result of possible kidney failure? How positive can you be with bipolar disorder knowing you might either have to give up Lithium or deal with organ failure?

Answer...These questions are valid and make a solid point. I would answer them by sharing my past life in depth with you, and showing that learning positivity is one of the most powerful tools when dealing with the challenges of bipolar disorder.

Let me begin with an article written in the winter 2007 issue of Bipolar Magazine: *Five Generations -- Understanding the Past -- Building the Future* by Donna Jackel.

Bipolar Disorder cast a long shadow over Dr. Fred's family. His grandmother, father, sister, two aunts, and several first cousins had the disorder. Fred, his identical twin Ted, and his only son, Todd, were diagnosed as well. What made Dr. Fred's family story one of hope is that thanks to improvements in treatment and attitudes towards mental illness, each successive generation has found it easier to achieve emotional stability.

Fifty years ago, Fred's father, Howard, could not reveal his struggles to anyone outside the family. Even his wife did not acknowledge his illness. Today, his grandson, Todd, a pastor at the time, felt comfortable sharing his diagnosis with his entire congregation. Howard, the Superintendent of Parks and Forestry for a large city in Indiana, was a respected figure. He was a frequent speaker at local gatherings, talking about care and importance of public parks. Also an expert on plants and the Bible, he spoke at local churches on the topic. He provided for his wife and four children and, like many others who struggled with Bipolar Disorder in the pre-Lithium era, he tried to cope with his extreme mood swings while keeping his illness a secret. When dark periods hit, Howard could not work for two or three weeks at a time.

"I remember a very conscientious, loving, giving person who always wanted to help his family," says Fred, a retired Optometrist living in Naples, Florida. "He was always there for us. Even if he was in a depressed state, he would go to our football game and hide the fact that he was in a depression."

During manic phases, Howard turned his unstoppable energy outside the home, working long hours. "As I was growing up, I could see he was having mood swings, but I didn't understand it. Neither did my brother," Fred recalled. "You expect a father to be consistent with love and affection, but with hypomania you are doing so many things."

Fred was 16 when he suffered his first major depression. He was having trouble with math and his grades were falling. "I didn't know it was depression," he says. "I just didn't feel like going to school -- I would vomit up my breakfast on the way..." To make matters worse, Ted did well in math without much effort. "I always felt very insecure about that." Fred says.

The twins were opposites in other ways. While Fred was shy, Ted was more aggressive and spoke loudly, even talking back to his father at times. Ted had a steady girlfriend throughout high school, while Fred barely dated. At the time, Ted did not yet suffer from depression. Yet they remained close.

The twins, who were also close to their father, suffered a great loss in 1962 when Howard died of a massive heart attack at age 52. Fred and Ted were 20. Soon after, Ted fell and broke his back while working on a construction site. He severed some nerves, permanently losing sensation in his lower abdominal area. The after-effects of Ted's back injury added to Fred's stress and depression and made it more difficult for him to cope with his bipolar disorder.

That same year, the twins entered the Indiana University School of Optometry in Bloomington, Indiana, but Fred fell into another depression his first year, which began to overwhelm him. "I was losing sleep and falling behind in classes." he says. "The stresses were way too high for me. I was afraid I would flunk out of school."
At the dean's suggestion, he decreased the number of courses he was taking. Fred also moved out of the fraternity house, where he had been subjected to hazing, and into a dorm. With these changes, his mood and his grades improved.

Turbulent Times

As the two young adults turned into men, Fred's life became more settled. He met his future wife, on a blind date. They connected right away. In her, he found the encouragement and sensitivity he had needed. "She had a tremendous ability to see when I needed help. Ted didn't have that." Fred and Linda were wed in 1964. As Fred found love, Ted's long-time relationship ended and then he too began to struggle with mood swings.

Two years later, Fred joined an Optometric practice in Detroit metropolitan area, Michigan, while Ted joined one in St. Louis, Missouri. In what he later realized was a burst of manic energy, Fred took on a second job as a visual consultant for the public schools, working a total of 80 hours a week. The grueling pace led him to another severe depression, which lasted about a year.

I found it very difficult to go to the office and see patients. I felt fatigued all the time," he recalls. "My self-confidence diminished markedly; I started to question whether I was qualified to be an optometrist".

So, Fred quit the school program but then, almost overnight, he was back in high gear-- getting by on three hours of sleep. Some nights he would go to the bar for a couple of drinks before heading home. Looking back, he now acknowledges he was self-medicating.

"When Fred was manic, he became a person I didn't know and who was hard to live with," Linda says. "It was lonely, it was difficult, and there were long hours not knowing where he was." Fred not only had a patient wife, but also a tolerant optometry partner. "He knew when I was in a depression and was gracious enough to let me work at my own pace." he says. But Fred, when manic, refused his partner's help. "I was very outspoken and opinionated," he recalls." I would say, 'I'm productive. I'm doing great.'" He now realizes that during those manic periods, he was abrupt with a few patients. "I was going too fast; I just wanted to see as many patients as I could."

In 1970, Fred was diagnosed with bipolar disorder (or manic-depression as it was known then). There were no mood stabilizers, so the psychiatrist prescribed antipsychotics, which carried unpleasant side effects. He discontinued all his medications and mania resumed.

Linda was six months pregnant with their daughter, Lisa, their son Todd was only three, when Fred was hospitalized to try out a new drug that had just been approved by the Food and Drug Administration (FDA) for the treatment of manic-depression--Lithium. He was in the hospital for six weeks as his psychiatrist tinkered to get the Lithium level correct. By the time Fred left the hospital in May of 1971, he felt "more normal" than he had in a long time. The psychiatrist told him he would have to take Lithium the rest of his life.

Fred was initially faithful about swallowing his daily pills, but after three years, he began secretly reducing the dosage. "I remembered very well the creativeness I had during a mania," he says. "Mania is like a drug--you are addicted to it." He began to slip back into old ways--working from early in the morning until 8 p.m. "Linda was very aware of what was going on," he says. "She could see I was becoming manic again: the rambling speech, staying out later at night, not following through with family chores."

His ability to parent was also affected when he was not taking his medication. "I was not a good father when they were young children," he says. "When I had mania, my attitude was, 'Linda can take care of them' I played with them when I was home, which wasn't too much, and it bothers me to this day."

Although Fred and Ted lived in separate cities, they remained close. By the early 1970s, Ted had been diagnosed with bipolar disorder.
In February 1978, Ted confided to his

brother that he was in a severe depression. Fred urged him to try Lithium but Ted said that he could not tolerate it. Instead, he went into the hospital for electroconvulsive therapy (ECT).

Darkest Days

The mood swings and the loss of sensation from his back injury wore Ted down until "he got to a place where nothing could solve his problems." Fred says. On April 25, 1978, just three days after their 36th birthday, Ted fatally shot himself, leaving a wife and three young children.

"I was devastated," Fred says. "The next three to four weeks, I was walking around in a deep dense fog. I could not believe my identical twin was dead."

After Ted's suicide, Fred began taking Lithium regularly. Still deeply grieving, he threw himself into tennis, racquetball, and especially running. He ran daily and competed in two marathons. "Exercise became a release for me," he recalls. "It seemed to control my mood swings."

But after four years of stability, Fred again went off his Lithium and the cycles repeated: mania followed by a deep, long depression. When he visited his mother, she criticized him for being down. After he returned home, he was so depressed he went to bed for two days. He could not face up to the fact that he and his mother would never have a close, meaningful relationship. Says Fred: "I kept trying to make it right".

But six years and one month after Ted's suicide, Fred took an overdose of antidepressants. Linda rushed him to the hospital. She was frustrated and angry. "I did not understand why he was not helping himself. I thought: 'there has to be a solution here', she says. While Fred was hospitalized, Linda and his medical team tried to figure out why he kept relapsing. Linda relayed how Fred's depression always seemed to worsen after a visit to his mother. "She did not want to listen to Fred when he wanted her to learn about bipolar disorder," Linda says of her mother-in-law. She was denying it happened at all."

The psychiatrist advised Fred to cut off all contact with his extended family-- including his mother. "When he broke away from them, we started working better as a family," says Linda.

As for Ted's violent death, it took several years for Fred to fully grieve for his twin. "If it were not for Linda I would not be here," he says simply.

As a couple, and separately, Linda and Fred began attending psychotherapy where Linda learned to be more assertive. "I had been enabling Fred to go off his Lithium by calling his office to say he was sick with the flu and trying to protect him," she says. And Fred began to listen more to his wife's point of view and be less domineering. He has remained on Lithium--initially with his wife's help. "When he came out of the hospital, I put the Lithium in a shot glass by his tooth brush," Linda says. And for five years, she stood right there until he swallowed those pills. "We had gone through 20 years of ups and downs and I decided I would not go through that again," she explains.

The past 28 years have been much calmer for Dr. Fred and Linda, who now have been married for 48 years. "With my stability, we have a beautiful life and we hope to have many more years that way." Fred says. The couple also experienced the joy of seeing their children marry and begin to raise their own families.

Moving Forward

Fred had a rare chance to help his son avoid some of the pain he endured as a young man. Ten years ago, Todd was in his first ministerial position, working alongside a senior pastor who had been at the church for 30 years and did not welcome new ideas. "It was like, 'this is my gig and don't mess with it,' and that was a great stress," Todd says. Feeling powerless, Todd first became depressed, and then manic. His family noticed the telltale symptoms, but broaching the subject was ticklish.

Fred asked his son to meet for coffee. "He had rapid speech and a lot of projects going all at once," Fred recalls. He says, "You probably think I'm manic." I said, "Yes". That really upset him. Fred suggested that Todd see a psychiatrist for an evaluation. Once he overcame his anger, Todd took his father's advice and has been stable on Lithium since.

The young man looks back at the lives of his grandfather, father and uncle, and appreciates that he has not had to endure what they did. "I am a beneficiary of my family's experiences," he says. "I am saddened that so many generations had to go through the pain and suffering they did. For some families, it is still under wraps."

Chapter 2:

Choices That Had to be Made

So, this personal story gives us an understanding of the very difficult past that I was able to overcome. It gave me an edge in developing a full positive attitude with bipolar disorder. We know that some people reject positive thinking because they perceive their life negatively. What they do not realize is that positive thought is a 'choice'. The person choosing often has experience with the dark side of things and that is why they have made the 'choice' to be positive.

A lot of people assume that if they are going to be negative, then something outside of them will give them a reason not to be that way. So they wait and wait and wait for something...and meanwhile in their minds they turn into shadows. They do not understand that if they wanted to see the world as beautiful, then they have only to make that 'choice' and stick by it.

Q...Give me examples of times where you made 'choices' to be positive, even though it seemed impossible?

A...This is a sad story, but still one of redemption. I hope it will help others when dealing with their bipolar disorder and to know that their life, too, can change for the better even after a sad event.

After 34 years have gone by, I still miss my brother, but his death was not in vain. For I have achieved over 28 years of "episode free emotional stability" with bipolar disorder. Perhaps a large number of people want an identical twin in their life, maybe because it fills a need to be themselves "twice over". That is a positive need because it makes them feel that if one of them is at fault (for anything), the other will not be. It is not the look-alike (glasses, clothes, facial expressions, or hairline) that identifies identical twins. It is what lies inside of them: a double soul that contains a deep knowledge of who each one of them really is--in reality, their identity.

I had that privilege for a short while, to live with my identical twin. But, 34 years ago, a biochemical imbalance took him away from me. You cannot escape your own attitudes, for they will form the nature of what you see. And those attitudes may always control a negative image of your past, if you permit it. I chose to look to the future and have my identical twin lead me to my own bipolar stability, fighting the same biochemical imbalance that we both shared. He and I are still the same, but also very different. Because I am alive, he is not. However, some of him is still with me. There was a choice I had to make, to climb out of that dark side of my life and to overcome a very personal loss and make it into a positive. My twin's death provided redemption, pushing me toward building my positive attitude, so he did not die in vain.

I am reminded of some simple decisions and choices I needed to learn while trying to replace the grieving of my brother's death. I found that my thoughts were clouded and that it seemed the devil, at times was a voice of reason. "Do this," the voice says, "and life will be easy for you. Do this and don't think about anything else. Do this and forget all that foolishness of serving others, sacrificing your time." Perhaps we need to leave where we are and venture forth in faith. It is a journey filled with decisions and choices. Filled, I dare say, with temptation and mood swings. The mark of a maturing spirituality, it seems to me, is the willingness to continue facing up to these alternatives, allowing ourselves to be changed, allowing ourselves to reason with positive thinking, to continue positive choices along this journey with bipolar disorder. Working through sickness, physically or mentally, provides a helpful perspective. Although I wish I could find an easier way of going about it, I am grateful for choosing a positive viewpoint.

I recall two days recently that had gone by in a blur. A patchy depression and a fever caused 48 hours to come and go, without much attention at all. Of course, you don't have to be sick to have that happen. Indeed, too often, too many of us fail to cherish each day, each hour and each minute. We find ourselves ignoring the richness of the life around us as we narrowly limit our focus to just our own lives. Those days indicated that the world goes along just fine without me. But I like being engaged with the world. I like participating in the lives that are all around me. I like getting up each day and heading off to meaningful activities and rewarding relationships. It seems to me, even on the edge of this miserable bipolar disorder, that these are the marks of the fulfilled life. It's not how much I've acquired, but rather whether I've managed to cherish life or not, all of life.

It became a source of enlightenment when the fever dissipated and that patchy depression began to lift because I was determined to practice "self help." However, the night after recovering, I dreamed of my dying. Actually, it may not have been a dream as much as that strange and mysterious time of transition between consciousness and unconsciousness. I seemed able to control the course of it and I stretched it out for a very long time. I remember I was weeping. I was surrounded by those I love and one by one, I was able to tell them what they meant to me. Slowly, I spoke of the gifts they had given me, the joy that we shared. When it was over, I lay in bed enjoying my tears and pondered again the things that really mattered. The knowledge of being able to find those positive choices and putting them to solid use will continue to guide me on those positive paths to overcome bipolar disorder.

Chapter 3:

Marriage and its Strengths

Q...How do you feel that your marriage was a very important aspect in your life in developing a positive attitude toward bipolar disorder?

A...Let me illustrate a few examples of my marriage as it relates to my struggles with bipolar disorder and my goal toward achieving episode free emotional stability. I will start by sharing a little story about my wife, Linda. She recalled in the spring of 1984, when I was in a very deep depression; I took the overdose of pills. When I was released from the hospital, she came to me with a message of "tough love". She said, "You need to start taking full responsibility for your life, or I'm going to leave you". It was a real wake up call for me. So I started that long hard journey, with bipolar disorder, to stability. Now, looking back, it was because of Linda, and developing a positive attitude, that I have succeeded with these years of stability.

Recently, as Linda and I were relaxing in our lanai, overlooking a small lake and a waterfall, I observed a few changes in her face that only come with time. However, those changes soon seemed to melt away with her radiant smile. The same smile she had since the day she was 22 and we wed.

How and why we came to be in love, I do not think either of us can say, but we both agree that staying in love takes a lot of work. The discipline of spending time together, of sharing activities, of listening to each other, of confessing our faults and forgiving each other---this is the work of staying in love. There are rituals of daily affection, daily household duties, and daily reminders of what it means to be in love...these are the means by which we nurture and sustain our relationship. To pray only when we felt like it, to dismiss duty or discipline as an archaic concept, is to court spiritual disaster.

A number of years ago, I received a Christmas card from an old friend who had attended Optometry school with me. Beneath the printed inscription that wished us a Merry Christmas, my friend had scribbled. "You two are the only ones left." It took me a few minutes to decipher the hidden message and then sadly it dawned on me what he meant. My wife and I were the only couple out of ten from those post-graduate years who had remained married. One out of ten! It hardly seemed possible. I sat and thought of all the pain that our friends had endured as their relationships came to an end. I thought of all the good times and bad times we had shared together as we trudged on in our academic careers. The dreams that we shared...all of it passed now as one relationship after another dissolved into divorce. What had happened that tore our friends apart? Perhaps more important, why had my wife and I been spared? We've spent years building our relationship through laughter and tears, good times and bad. But we both were determined to fulfill future hopes and unrealized dreams. Why has it worked so far?

I am convinced that there are a number of factors that keep the flame burning between Linda and myself not the least of which is the realization of the tenuous nature of the flame. How easily it can flicker and fade. How quickly it can be blown out. Each time my wife and I struggled through my episodes of bipolar disorder, we were reminded of all the outside forces that could wreak havoc with our married life. Jobs, money, and children...these are just some of the pressures that can, at the wrong moment, blow like a gale against the flame and threaten to extinguish it. These are the times when we nurture the flame even as those outside forces seek to blow it out. To recognize that flickering fragility is to guard against the darkness of separation and divorce. These were the times I needed most to develop a positive attitude.

A strong marriage is the result of kindness, simple kindness. It seems so elementary and yet so many find it elusive. A gentle word, an inquiring look, a surprising hug...they did wonders for myself and Linda. And the joy of it all is that it is so very much fun to do! These are not painful, difficult actions. Kindness is so easy and the rewards are so great, I am amazed I did not see it more often. I remain convinced that the healing and strengthening power of kindness is one answer to the stability of marriage and ultimately my bipolar disorder. The continuing fulfillment of our marriage works like an ever-developing globe to protect our flame. Such faithfulness allows us the freedom to share fully in each other's lives. And now I can continue to see a trend here of 'choice' toward positive thinking in my life. It truly was a 'choice' that had to be. Bipolar Disorder is difficult enough to deal with, but living a married life without positive thoughts to keep the negative symptoms of bipolar at bay, can be insurmountable.

Chapter 4:

Environment, Genetics, and Family Unity

Q...Are there other factors that influence your "choice" toward staying positive with bipolar disorder?

A...Environment and genetics, along with family unity, are as important in a strong and stable marriage to maintain a positive attitude.

Most all of us know that bipolar disorder is a genetic/inherited disorder. I have long wondered how parent's personalities and emotions play with their offspring, as to the degree of onset with bipolar disorder. Expressed emotion (EE), defined as emotionally intrusive, critical and hostile comments from various family members towards the person with the disorder, was one of the first variables demonstrated to influence the course of bipolar disorder. The effective size for EE in bipolar disorder is significant. The detrimental effects of EE are more pronounced when received from parents than from a marital partner. Low maternal warmth is a risk factor for relapse in adolescent bipolar patients. In bipolar disorder, EE holds predictive power even after accounting for subsyndromal symptoms and personality traits. Family members who may feel unconsciously or consciously responsible for the offspring's disorder (e.g., either through bad genes and/or adverse rearing environments), or see symptoms as under the patient's control, may be more prone to blame the patient and feel angry towards him/her.

I ask, could parental and environmental influence help off-set bipolar disorder? Every two years we have our extended family reunion. I am the patriarch of this reunion. Between my brother and sisters and their children, we have 18 kids, ages four to 15 years in the third generation. An interesting fact is that there are four members in the first generation that had bipolar, five members in the second generation and one member in the third generation. So, it is obvious that the genetics of bipolar are involved within my family.

As I watch this third generation of children play and react with each other, my mind could not help but think and feel, "Which one will be the next child with bipolar ?" Then it dawned on me that parental and environmental influence is a large part or percentage of bipolar disorder. And if the parents play it right, could these 18 kids just somehow escape the wrath of the past?

There have been repeated findings that between a third and a half of adults diagnosed with bipolar disorder report traumatic experiences in childhood, which is associated on average with earlier onset. The total number of reported stressful events in childhood is higher in those with an adult diagnosis of bipolar disorder, compared to those without—particularly events stemming from a harsh environment rather than from the child's own behavior. Children can be like tape recorders or parrots. They mimic or repeat what they hear, and more importantly what they see or observe. This is true for behavior, attitude, and the formation of morals and lifestyle choices. The following text, from an unknown author, describes this point very well. The poem can serve as a guide for parents, who must make sure that they realize that teaching is not only verbal, but non-verbal too:

"If children live with criticism, they learn to condemn.
If children live with hostility, they learn to fight.
If children live with ridicule, they learn to be shy.
If children live with shame, they learn to feel guilty.
If children live with tolerance, they learn to be patient.
If children live with encouragement, they learn confidence.
If children live with praise, they learn to appreciate.
If children live with fairness, they learn justice."

Neil Moonie reminds us: If children live with security, they learn to have faith. He goes on to say, "If children live with approval, they learn to like themselves. If children live with acceptance and friendship, they learn to find love in the world."

Again, I keep suggesting that the 'choice' of being positive with bipolar is the direction to pursue. Family gatherings continue to build the foundation of positive thinking. Another positive example of family influence with bipolar disorder.

There is an old oak table. It is stained and marked from over a hundred years of daily use. It has five leaves that allow it to expand to seat 14 people quite comfortably or 20 slightly squeezed. It has an interesting history. Although there's no label underneath, I've been able to track its history back as far as the turn of the century in Berne, Indiana. It originally came from a community from Gunten, Switzerland. It belonged to my great grandfather, who was a prominent individual in a not-so prominent town. He and his wife took great pride in raising their family. As the family grew, each child, grandchild, and great-grandchild took pride in carving their names underneath this great oak table. I can remember the laughter and loving fellowship that was shared.

In any case, it is a fine old table. Sturdy and well-built, to be sure, but its substance comes, I am convinced, not so much from the oak as from the occasions that it served as host to. It was, without question, the center of our family life...or at least the place where our family centers. It is a symbol and a reminder to all of us what it means to be a positive family. It is a place of relationships and it is as holy as any altar could ever be.

Being able to find the everyday simplicity in our lives is something to behold. Bipolar Disorder can eat away the daily moods that fall upon us. I learned about this simplicity years ago with my son as we walked together. I was looking for those positive answers to give insight into my always present bipolar. As he hiked with me through golden leaves by a hidden mountain lake, we were left peacefully to sit and watch the wind breathe on the water and overhear the gossip chattered among squirrels and their neighbors. We spoke, in that wonderfully unspoken way, my son and I. We shared our dreams in silence sitting by the mountain lake. We talked of the future and of what he would remember of this time when he was four and his dad was 30 and they went for a hike on a brilliantly blue day. We prayed with our hearts that God would remind us of this holy time of father and son and we laughed without making a sound as we cherished the moment together.

I was susceptible to images of time that day, for I still struggled with my bipolar episodes. I stood with feet firmly planted on the ground and watched as time had raced by me and had an uncanny feeling that my son would one day have to tackle this same disorder. Until, by a hidden mountain lake, God reminded me of who I am and where I am rapidly heading. He hugged me, my son did. In a gesture that was very briefly startling as we sat together and alone by the water. It was a warm reminder that angels often disguise themselves as children. We were held together by love and our rhythmic breathing, gracefully hypnotized. "Time and tide wait for no man," but occasionally they slow down to a crawl and you find yourself breathing a little easier, breathing with your son.

And now as time has passed, the simplicity continues with my grandson. I thank God that my "choice'" toward positive thinking has continued to support my stability. Perhaps, as I have achieved stability in my life with bipolar disorder, I am able to live a more positive life and enjoy the "small stuff". I was thinking about this lack of mindfulness from which so many of us suffer. I recall a time last winter when I was walking with my little grandson and we stopped by a bridge to watch the water from a small creek flow through the ice and snow. We crouched for a while paying particular attention to an icicle slowly letting go--drop after drop of clear, pristine water. Finally, the little boy spoke. "Papa," he said, "why are you so good to me?" I suspect that he was sensing the holiness of the moment. I have a hunch that he realized just how rarely we adults stop to watch water flow or icicles drip. I needed to come to terms with the genetics that may encompass my bipolar disorder and my grandchildren. What to do? I do expect to be positive and honest with them.

A child is only interesting if he is in contact with himself. I learned you have to trust yourself, be what you are, and do what you ought to do the way you should do it. You have got to discover you, what you do, and trust it. Facing a mirror, you see merely your own countenance; facing your grandchild, you finally understand how everyone else has seen you. Grown-ups never understand anything for themselves, and it is tiresome for children to be always and forever explaining things to them. We must level with our children and grandchildren by being honest. No one spots a phony quicker than a child. A child of five would understand this....Send someone to fetch me a child of five.

Chapter 5:

Changes That Had to be Made

Q...Are there more than environmental, genetics and family unity that build your strengths of positive thinking?

A...The simple fact is that "change" is needed in every person's life to continue with positive growth.

It is over 13 years ago that I started a new phase of my life (Since Jan.1999). It included retirement, contentment and enhancement of stability with bipolar disorder. Have any of you thought that the retired mind could free you from the constant biochemical changes that cause bipolar disorder? Perhaps it is the changes in environment that relaxes the mind in retirement. Therein lies a possible answer to enhancing stability.

We all know from our sessions with the

psychiatrist, that change of space and surrounds can give relaxation to mind and body. For example: lying flat on your back, under a warm sunlit beach in Florida. Often times, it is just a simple change in environment that will melt some of the threats of mood change. Five years into my retirement, I knew that I needed more "contentment and "enhancement" in my life, and continued growth toward my stability. I had achieved my goal of stability with Lithium for the past 15 years before retirement. However, there was still a deeper need to find a change of environment to soothe the balance of bipolar disorder.

So it was that my wife and I left Michigan for Naples, Florida, eight years ago.
I share these thoughts, because I believe that any environmental change can be a tremendous factor in controlling stability with bipolar. Quite often I have heard from others that "If only I could get away somewhere, I know that these feelings and moods would change." It is a wonder, my friends, that life with stability may be just around the corner, at a different place that you can call a "Paradise of the Mind".

To answer the questions why I feel it is so important to maintain a positive attitude with bipolar disorder, I felt that I needed to "change" so many areas in my life. The negative symptoms with bipolar required a positive change in dealing with everyday demands. These are some of the positive changes I have made in my life in the last 28 years:

-Change my concept of 'pride.' I had too much feeling of honor. I was too 'puffed' up.
-Change speech patterns. My tone of voice carried a sound of dominance, meanness, and rudeness. I needed to learn how to speak softly.
-Change my point of view. I carried an 'air' of always being 'right'.
-I would always counter others points of view. Made them feel worthless/useless.
-I needed to let go of having to win an argument.
-Difficult to admit a mistake.
-Using a 'sarcastic' type of humor.
-Change listening habits to become a better listener.
-Change conversation habits. Would always interrupt or 'talk over' what others were saying.
-Change the way I think, so that my life may change.
-Change or suspend my 'pomposity' and 'rigidity' so others could recognize my 'flexibility' and be able to find trust in

me.

-I needed to let go of 'striving'. To change how I may be viewing the present. To change how I view 'striving', then to develop 'contentment' without anxiety and fear.

-Change how I would act and react with others. Be in charge of emotions by trying not to fly off the handle.

-Change to be responsible for all my 'actions'.

-Change and /or control 'ego', inwardly, for more self-esteem, self-control, and self- confidence.

With these 'changes' I was able to build on my "Power of Positivity" with bipolar disorder.

When trying to always point to the positive for bipolar, might I suggest that one critical aspect I have learned is to not ask people for "advice" but rather to seek their "opinion." It was one of those moments when you slap yourself on the forehead and say "why the heck couldn't I have thought of it that way?" It is such an important distinction, and asking for advice creates pressure because there is an implicit risk of "what if my advice is wrong," whereas, if you ask me for my opinion, the risk feels much, much less. "We all have opinions, and actually like to express them."

Another very important quality of communication was "pausing" before interfering. I now would deliberately bite my tongue and zip my lips at the precise moment that I was tempted to get involved in the lives of those around me. I needed to become aware of my inclination to tell others, particularly my family members how they should be conducting their lives. Even if I hold off for a few moments before I interfere in someone else's business, I would be on my way to allowing those around me to find their anchor within themselves. This new discipline of resisting the habit to get involved by "pausing" before I would be interfering, enabled me to see how capable everyone truly is when they are in the energy field of someone who "allows" rather then "dictates."

Learning that faith is a gift from God, then, this kind of faith is God's gift to me. But in the words of that great theologian and spinach-fed sailor..."I yam who I yam and that's all I can be." Have those of us with bipolar disorder continued to be all we can be? Have we all truly accepted our diagnosis? And do we have that faith that we can achieve stability?

To help build my faith with God, I needed to find more simplicity. I felt there was a concerted need to "change" my physical activity.

I have begun a new type of walk, two or three times a week. I call it a "soul walk;" entirely different than my physical walk that I do three or four times a week:

-While engaged in soul walking, one should let one's mind simply relax. Soul walks are not undertaken in order to solve life's problems, resolve difficult situations or decide future activities.

-Soul walks are simply for walking.
-If you are accustomed to timing your walks or using a pedometer then this kind of walking will be a new experience for you.
-If you are one of those curious folk who have taken up the latest and strange fad of aerobic walking...soul walking may take some getting used to.
-As I am out on a soul walk, all kinds of wonderful things happen. A porcupine ambles on. Squirrels stop by to say hello. The sun rises. Ducks fly by in slow motion. These are wonderful things that remind me of why I live near the warm Gulf of Mexico winds. Indeed, why I live

at all.

-I am convinced that we need a little less regimen to our living and a lot more purposeless activity...like soul walking.

-Which brings me to my final point and, I believe, it brings out the positive thinking in us that have bipolar. It is the relaxation that we so often need. It is strictly for fun.

-If you become compulsive about it or develop a daily discipline that demands your allegiance, then it is not soul walking anymore; it is something else, and it may even be good for you, but it is definitely not soul walking.

-Soul walking is an exercise in nothingness. There is no purpose, no destination, no reward but the walk itself.

It is from the soul walking experience, that I began to wonder what other exploratory events could happen with my bipolar life. It was then that I recalled when I was in the "wilderness" of depression, that I discovered positivity of "change" to be free. It was there that I formed and firmed up my potential goals to overcome potential episodes. Sadly, and too often, our negativity tells us precisely the opposite. It says, "Don't change. Don't grow. Don't do anything different than what has been done before. So often we people with bipolar disorder, are in a "wilderness" all our own. The question is? Can we "change" and grow so that we can be free from our own "wilderness?" Things get shaken up in the "wilderness." That is when I found my answers were to "change" from my old ways and to continue to work with my doctors, my prescribed Lithium, my family, and developing a higher level toward positivity.

Sometimes I wonder if the reason we so easily pray not to be led into temptation is because we are so very comfortable where we are. In the midst of everything else going on in our lives, the last thing we want is to confront the possibility of "change." "Lead us not into temptation" may be just another way of saying, "Look, my life may not be perfect but at least it's familiar, so please God don't complicate it with invitations into the unknown." Surely we face similar temptations. We are tempted to convince ourselves that we are doing all we can for God and for others...and perhaps we are...but why then are we, as people with bipolar disorder, so afraid to hear of other possibilities? Why are we so uncomfortable when the invitation to "change" is placed before us?
Is it because we are afraid to discover

who we really are?

Chapter 6:

Knowing God's Love

Q...What would you say is the ultimate direction you needed to turn to after you started those changes in your life?

A...There are times in anyone's life that we need to look deeply into the spiritual realm, whether we find comfort in nature or a Super-Human. Religion is the belief in a Super-Human power or divine entity, usually referred to as God. It is expressed in worship and manifests as a spiritual experience. A Super-Human being may have great power, along with nature and all human affairs. And so, God is not the exclusive property of our spiritual needs. Nature, Christians, Zion, Islam, Buddha or whoever, may be the common choice for each of our individual needs. I happen to choose God. I have found comfort and support with His positive guidance in my life.

Perhaps, my soul walking has given me a relaxed, deeper insight into God's gift of Love. Someone once said, "Love is not a feeling, it is a policy." Love is a way of life. If we really desire the abiding presence of God, then we must abide by all the consequences of that presence as well. It means there will be deep joy in our lives but it also means that this joy will emerge only as we give joy to others. It means there will be the recognition that God is truly our friend, but it also means that we are called into friendship with others. It means that life will be abundant and rich, but it also means that this abundance will come only as we empty ourselves and give freely of our richness to others who need our gifts.

To be a friend of God is to live in this paradox. To walk with the reality that following God, will mean going places we never thought we wanted to go. It is to discover the deep peace that can be ours when we are truly willing to have the presence of God abiding amongst us. It is that ultimate, 'positive walk' down the "road less travelled" with bipolar disorder to our stability with God!

The wonder of this life is that we are free to choose how we are to live it. We are free to choose what paths we will take. We choose whether we wish to live with paralyzing guilt or the promise of always cultivating the positive aspects of life. We choose whether we wish to live a life to conform or to be free. We choose!

This is precisely the point we need to decide. We don't need to follow the rules in order to please God. God gives us the rules in order to please us. Living lives of chastity, kindness and mercy is not done so that God will love us. God loves us now and gives these gifts. If we choose not to open them up, not to utilize them in our lives, then we live with the consequences. In our freedom, we may enter into the wrath of multiple bipolar episodes, or choose the road less travelled to stability. We choose!

While keeping the journey positive and keeping my goals high in helping people with bipolar, I ask myself what successes have I had? Perhaps it is my example of stability in my own life that proves the symptoms of bipolar can be conquered. Of course, there is my history of 28 years of episode free emotional stability. Is it because I just lucked out with one mood stabilizer, Lithium? Is it because of a loyal and loving wife and family? Is it because I needed to confront the bipolar demons that possessed my extended family history? Is it because I continue to develop a positive attitude and self image of who I am as a person who knows that my life is as "normal" as everyone else's life? My answer is yes!

God and the concepts of spirituality have given me the love and support I continue to need. It is my friends with bipolar that are a constant encouragement. Most every one of them who struggle with bipolar daily, are looking for the correct answers to their own stability. A few have achieved it most are still suffering for directions. I know that positive hope can be their answer. It is ultimately up to all of them to follow that positive journey; to know that God is always present to guide them.

If only I believed more that this thorn of bipolar disorder would be removed, I once thought and with such thinking the pain grew even more pronounced. But then I realized that even here, God could work. Even with the pain, even with the burden. Indeed, it was through this thorn that my faith grew stronger. It was here that I began to understand the paradox of this strange and wondrous faith of ours. In weakness we are made strong. In defeat comes victory. To love a world that often hates us, to forgive those who turn their backs, to offer charity when what we are tempted to do is hoard our gifts. In these acts of foolishness and failure, come the miracles of God.

We miss out on God when we expect God's appearance to come only in success, victory, and power. More often, God comes in the quiet acts of kindness, mercy and grace, in the midst of the ordinariness of our lives. I was relieved that these quiet times often came in my depression. But, somehow I always could feel the presence of God. I knew He was there to lift me into positive thinking.

Surely one of the reasons "Field of Dreams" was such a big hit a decade or so ago was this desire all of us have for God to speak to us. If only God would give me a word like he did for Kevin Costner out there in that field of dreams. Why doesn't God speak to me the way God has done for others? God does all the time, only we need to listen. "I will not leave you desolate. I will come to you," He says. And he does. He comes in many ways.

Someone once said that God knocks on

the door. God doesn't break it down. I needed to open the door and let God in. I needed to learn how to listen to the voice that calls to me in many different ways, using many different voices.

I now listen to God. He has given me the positive answers to deal with the triggers causing potential episodes. Perhaps, God knows bipolar disorder better than I do. So I listen carefully for His positive voice, and know that I have fulfilled my dreams toward stability.

Chapter 7:

Influential People with Positive Thoughts

Q...Are there others who have encouraged you to choose positive thinking and have given you the knowledge that your own mental health is part of controlling your actions? Could you share how your experiences with these people have encouraged you to stay positive with bipolar?

A...There are many stories from over the years that have encouraged me forward to maintain the stability that I now have. These stories come from people who have experienced their own struggles with mental disorders, and from those who feel that need to motivate everyone with positive remarks and stories that we can live by on a daily basis.

There are many engines that pull the

train of mental health technology. One
highly accredited resource is NAMI
(National Alliance of Mental Illness).
NAMI is the nation's largest grassroots
mental health organization dedicated to
improving the lives of people living with
mental illness and their families.
Founded in 1979, NAMI has become the
nation's voice on mental illness. A
national organization including NAMI
organizations in every state and in over
1100 local communities across the
country who join together to meet the
NAMI mission through advocacy,
research, support, and education. It was
with the NAMI group sessions that I
learned and grew in my own self
confidence.

An inspiring story came in the month of
March a couple of years ago in Naples,
Florida. Not only was the morning crisp,
clear and warm, but it was that time
again for the "Annual NAMI WALK" with
this years theme "Un-masking Mental
Illness". The Grand Marshall was Joey
Pantoliano who experienced "euphoria"
after doctors diagnosed him with clinical
depression. Because he could finally
understand his feelings of despair, the
former Sopranos star, 57, was relieved
when his doctor pronounced this
diagnosis. This explained why he felt so

miserable, despite having the success he'd always dreamed of having. Since then he, who manages his depression with medication, has helped launch an organization called "No Kidding, Me Too (nkm2)" which aims to remove the stigma attached to mental illness. He says, "Mental disorder is the only thing you can be diagnosed with and get yelled at for having. Why is that?" "From the moment I was diagnosed there was a certain sense of euphoria and 'Thank God' we figured this out, because I thought that I'd become such a curmudgeon."

He ended his ten minute talk to all of us who were eager to start the three mile walk with this comment: "Remember if people ask who you are, be sure to tell the mental disorder you have." After he walked off the stage, "I told my wife I'm going to shake his hand." Well, I did more then that...I walked up to him, stuck out my hand and looked him in the eye and said "I'm Bipolar". He held my hand tight and said, "I was Depressed" and smiled. I continued by saying, "I have been stable for 25 years". He parted by saying, "Congratulations and keep telling everyone." With that, my wife and I walked the three miles in just under one hour, the fastest I have ever completed it. Perhaps it may be due to two new artificial knees, a new aortic replacement heart valve, continued Lithium medication and my own positive "Self Help".

Tibetan monks have a ritual time to make a sand mandala - so beautiful and then the wind blows it away and they return some of the sand to the river. The Naples News read:
January 16, 2005 - *Grain by Grain -Two Days Left, What It Is:* A Tibetan sand mandala created by monks from the Drepung Loseling Monastery, in Sanskrit, this particular "Akshobya" mandala symbolizes Healing and Indestructibility. The monks, who began making the mandala out of marble sand at the Naples, FL Museum of Art, completed the mandala over the next two days, meant to bring positive energies and healing to the Naples area. As I stood by watching, I asked one of the monks who waited to participate, "what will become of this?" He just smiled and stated "it is for you and you're healing". Then the day came. With a few swipes of a paintbrush, the brightly colored sand that had been a Tibetan mandala lay in a heap, a metaphor of the impermanence of life. Nine Tibetan Buddhist monks spent three days constructing the mandala from

millions of grains of exquisitely cultured sand, carefully laid into place on a black platform. Shortly after completing the mandala, the monks blessed it and dismantled it. Half of the sand was given to some people who came to watch, the other half went with the monks to the Naples Beach. There they carefully and blissfully placed the cultured sands into the Gulf of Mexico. I stood and watched a long time until most everyone was gone. A remaining monk came over and said to me, "Why do you stay...your mind is already healed." And somehow I knew it would always be.

M Scott Peck, M D states in his book *The Road Less Travelled* that: "I deviated from traditional psychiatry in that I located the source of psychiatric ills in the conscious mind, rather than the unconscious. It was the previous view, the Freudian sort of view, that the unconscious was filled with all these bad feelings, angry thoughts and sexy thoughts. That was where psychiatric, psychological illness originated. When in fact, the real question is why those things, which were obvious, were in the unconscious rather than the conscious mind. The answer was that it was a conscious mind that did not want to face certain truths, and pushed this stuff into the unconscious. But the problem is with a rejecting consciousness in which we simply don't like to think about things. Over the years I came to believe, and again I'm leaving out the biological aspects, that psychological disorders are all disorders of "thinking".

"So a narcissist, for instance, cannot or will not think of other people. What we used to call passive-dependent people cannot think for themselves. Obsessive-compulsive tend to have great difficulty thinking in the big picture. Bipolar Disorder tends to think that they will always have a mood shift in their lives. And I would say that if you have a patient or a client who has some real difficulty, psychological difficulty, then look for the problem in their 'thinking'. There is some area where they are not thinking correctly."

There was a gentleman, years ago, who most of you may not know much about because you are too young. He coached the Alabama "Crimson Tide" for 25 years from 1958 to 1982. His record wins, 323, have never been surpassed. His name was Paul William "Bear" Bryant. How does this coach's discipline of football relate to the discipline of handling bipolar disorder in positive ways? He states: "I have always tried to teach my players to be fighters. When I say that, I don't mean put up your dukes and get in a fistfight over something. I'm talking about facing adversity in your life. There is not a person alive who isn't going to have some awfully bad days in their lives. I tell my players that what I mean by fighting is when your house burns down, and your wife runs off with the drummer, and you've lost your job and all the odds are against you, what are you going to do? Most people just lie down and quit. Well, I want my people to fight back.

"Have a plan in your life and be able to adjust to it. Have a plan when you wake up, what you're going to do with your day. Never go lolly gagging through any day of your life. I hope I had some luck in my life because I have planned for the good times and the bad ones.

It's awfully important to win with humility. It's also important to lose. I hate to lose worse than anyone, but if you never lose you won't know how to act. If you lose with humility, then you can come back.
Losing doesn't make me want to quit. It makes me want to fight that much harder.

"Little things make the difference. Everyone is well prepared in the big things, but only the winners perfect the little things.

The first time you quit, it's hard. The second time, it gets easier. The third time, you don't even have to think about it.

There's a lot of blood, sweat, and guts between dreams and success.

"If you believe in yourself and have dedication and pride - and never quit - you'll be a winner. The price of victory is high but so are the rewards."

For now, you may understand how Coach Paul William "Bear" Bryant's positive attitude may answer some of the questions a bipolar needs to develop in organizational and coping skills, as they work toward being a "Functional Bipolar" with stability. Yes, not all those with bipolar can achieve this level of determination in order to fight the biochemical changes in their brains. However, it is worth the effort of acquiring that positive foundation to fight mood changes and the symptoms that trigger their occurrence.

In the last 12 years, I have had a recurrent dream. One that seems totally out of reach, but at times I know it is very real; because I lived it for 33 years when I was in practice. I am in a consultation room with my partners in practice. We are always in a deep discussion with each other. They are all talking and expressing their own opinions. And I am talking, however, I can not hear myself talk and they can not hear me either. The dream continues, but I am still not heard. So, the question is, why do I still have this dream after retirement of over 12 years? There had to be something I had to 'change', and it had to be me. Without those 'changes', the dream could not have ended. I could now hear myself and others could hear what I had to say. Perhaps, the question for each man/woman is to work on change. It is not what he/she would do if they had the means, time, influence and educational advantages; but the question is what they will do with the things they have. The moment a man ceases to bemoan his lack of opportunities and resolutely looks his conditions in the face, and resolves to 'change' them, he lays the cornerstone of a solid and honorable success. So, it was with that I found the importance of positive change for controlling my bipolar disorder.

This brings me to a childhood experience that taught me the basis of 'balance' with my bipolar. Life is like a teeter totter. When you need someone's help to make something work, and you have to place yourself in a position of vulnerability, it's important to pick someone you can trust, otherwise, they might just jump off and let you fall to the ground.

I can say I am always trying to balance the teeter-totter. I was not one of those kids who would run away when the other person was at the top. Remember going on the teeter-totters, and all the kids were taken, so you paired up with a bigger kid you did not know too well? And then all of sudden, he would jump off at the crucial moment and you would go 'slam' into the ground! And he would walk away laughing. Every kid learns this lesson, at least once. It taught me that very big lesson in achieving bipolar balance and that few are available to help you acquire that needed balance of mood swings. You have to be responsible for your own balance to achieve stability.

I have read Mitch Albom's *Have A Little Faith*. Albom's prose offers readers an elegantly simple perspective on faith, tolerance, service, and love while maintaining the complex reality of his characters' true life stories. I would like to share with you a sermon from the Jewish rabbi:

"A man seeks employment on a farm. He hands his letter of recommendation to his new employer. It reads simply, 'He sleeps in a storm'

"The owner is desperate for help, so he hires the man.

"Several weeks pass, and suddenly, In the middle of the night, a powerful storm rips through the valley.

"Awakened by the swirling rain and howling wind the owner leaps out of bed. He calls for his new hired hand, but the man is sleeping soundly.

"So he dashed off to the barn. He sees, to his amazement, that the animals are secure with plenty of feed.

"He runs out to the field. He sees the bales of wheat have been bound and are wrapped in tarpaulins.

"He races to the silo. The doors are latched, and the grain is dry.

"And then he understands...'He sleeps in a storm'.

"My friends, if we tend to the things that are important in life, if we are right with those we love and behave in line with

our faith, our lives will not be cursed with an aching throb of unfulfilled business. Our words will always be sincere, our embraces will be tight. We will never wallow in the agony of 'I could have, I should have.'
"And when it's time, our good-byes will be complete."

Perhaps, we with bipolar are advised to understand this concept. We need to think ahead, to develop a pattern in our lives and always pursue a positive attitude. The challenge is there--we must face it. Then we, too, can sleep in our own storm!

Chapter 8:

Using Positive Therapy

Q...Dr. Fred, there are still some health questions about the Lithium you are taking and the long term effects on your kidneys and thyroid. Perhaps, you may be "pushing the positive" with bipolar disorder a little too hard. How will you continue to address this concern?

A...Perhaps, it might be helpful to review how the brain responds to changes in its biochemistry. Evaluating these changes with the way moods may change, will give us the reasons why there may be an increase or decrease of bipolar symptoms.

Can the mind stave off disease? Growing evidence links positive thinking to a longer and healthier life. But, can simply thinking good thoughts help you deal with some of the ups and downs of bipolar disorder? Yes, how you think can often affect the way you feel and act. Bipolar Disorder is a brain disorder that causes swings between low mood and high. There are several different types, and people with bipolar vary widely in how severe their moods are. But in general, bipolar disorder is marked by emotional turmoil ranging from grandiose thinking to irritability and rage to sadness and feelings of worthlessness.

Bipolar is a serious condition that typically needs to be treated with both medication and psychotherapy. Therapy may help develop problem-solving strategies, how to communicate better, how to handle social situations and how to learn relaxation methods. This type of counseling called cognitive behavioral therapy or CBT, is designed to help people change negative, harmful thoughts and behavior patterns. There are other effective types of psychotherapy used to treat bipolar disorder, but let us focus on CBT.

Positive results with cognitive behavioral therapy, CBT, are a skills-oriented form of psychotherapy. In CBT, counselors teach tools to help manage moods, change thinking and cope with problems. For example, people are taught to recognize negative thinking patterns. These patterns often lead to problem behaviors and depressed moods. Some of these patterns include:

-All-or-nothing thinking.
-Thinking the worst will happen (can be self-fulfilling prophesy).
-Feeling others are thinking negative thoughts toward you (personalizing).

One may be coached on techniques to help gain some distance from these negative thinking habits. One tool is called "thought stopping." As its name implies, you literally tell yourself to stop when you are having irrational or automatic thoughts. Then replace the negative thoughts with more positive thoughts.

For example, your boss e-mails you to set up an appointment with you. You might automatically think: "I'm going to get fired. I won't be able to make my house payment." Or, "He doesn't like me. I'll never succeed in this job." In the past, you may have complained to co-workers about your boss before you even knew why he wanted the meeting. In CBT, you would be coached to replace the negative thoughts with something like "My boss wants an update on the project. Or I have done the best that I can at this job. Perhaps, he will give me the promotion I deserve".

Another tool is a "mood graph." By writing down your moods along with the factors that influenced them, you can identify situations that might make you more depressed or more manic.

Of course, finding the right therapist and committing to a consistent therapy schedule can be a hard feat in itself. Ask your doctor if he can suggest a licensed counselor who has training in CBT. It is important to find a therapist with whom you feel comfortable relaying your inner thoughts. Also, you must trust this person to give you honest feedback and value that feedback.

For many, learning how to cope with bipolar is a lifelong journey. CBT can help give you some of the tools needed for that journey. Learning how to think in a more positive manner might help you take some of the bumps out of life. Many times, we spend hours and hours dwelling on moods (mania) ruminating negative and fearful things in our lives. Instead, our focus and attention needs to be on the positive, the good; thoughts that will move us in the right direction.

Read one of these statements to yourself every day and dwell on it:

-If you pay attention to the darkness, you will never find the light. If you study and relive your past experiences, analyzing them, and "getting in touch with your feelings" you will only reinforce those feelings.

-One should not focus on negative. Focus on the good, the positive, the beautiful, and the nice. A happy person is fully caught up in the moment -- and is not thinking about the past or the future; too much thinking and analyzing just makes any problem worse. Today is a wonderful day--live it in the present.

-Why do little children think ghosts, goblins, and monsters are real? As adults, we know they are not. Your thoughts are not "real" either in the sense that you "create" and reinforce them -- and the emotions that go along with them. Your thoughts are only what you decide to believe in and continually reinforce in your mind. (This one is deep – think about this one.) For example, you are sitting alone in the dark in your home. You are down, depressed and thinking negative thoughts. All of a sudden the phone rings and it's a friend you haven't talked to in six years. You become alert, your mood picks up, and you have a nice conversation. Then, after you have hung up, you get blue again and fall back into a depressed mood. Why? Suggestion: Even though we don't feel it, we have more power over our thoughts than we think. We can decide to stay "up" after the phone call by doing everything we can to keep from slipping back into the quicksand of rumination and despair. (Cognitive-behavioral therapy gives us the tools to move away from anxiety and depression – and eventually to stay or "be" that way.) If your thoughts begin to change, you will feel better. If you act despite your feelings, your beliefs and emotions will follow behind.

-There is so much in life I cannot control. But this is my life and I have decided to be happy. I can choose to be happy regardless of my other circumstances. It is not when I get a promotion, I will be happy or when I can speak in front of a small group of people, I will be happy. The focus should be on learning to be happy now. Tap into your inner peace and contentment in the way that works best for you.

-Happiness is a result of a decision to be

happy.

-Your emotions and feelings are created by your thoughts.

-Unhappiness cannot exist on its own. It occurs because of thoughts, which can be changed.

Your past thoughts are about events that are no longer real. That bad experience happened yesterday (in the past) and is over. It is gone and exists solely in your mind. Today is a new day, a better day, and worrying about the past just dooms us in the present. It is how you process it now that makes a difference.

You are a thought-producing machine. When you realize this, you can begin to slow your thoughts down and allow your anxieties and fears to rest. Your automatic negative thoughts are only thoughts, they are not real, and they do not tell you the truth.

Long-term prevention of relapse into the manic or depressive episodes of bipolar disorder is our tendency to think too much and to paralyze ourselves with our ruminations. We have a choice: Realize what we are doing to ourselves, get up, find a distraction, do something interesting (positive).

Happy people understand that to enjoy life you live it -- you don't think about it.

Watch a roomful of preschool children. They are enjoying life because they are focused on the moment and are not thinking about it. They are immersed and absorbed in living.

Chapter 9:

Will Stability Last?

Q...What about long-term stability? Is it ever a possibility for a bipolar? How can it be achieved? And if it is even acquired, will it be retained?

A...I heard this quote a long time ago by Leonard Louis Levinson: "A pessimist sees only the dark side of the clouds, and mopes; a philosopher sees...both sides, and shrugs; an optimist does not see clouds at all - he is walking on them." We need to set higher standards for the emotional wellness and stability of people with bipolar disorder. On a personal basis, I believe that a "functional bipolar" needs to achieve "episode free emotional stability" to be productive.

Relapse can have devastating consequences for those with bipolar disorder. During relapse into mania or depression, they may experience disruptions in relationships and jobs, suffer feelings of failure or become suicidal.

A primary goal must be helping people with bipolar maintain health and well-being, not only treating episodes of bipolar as they arise, but preventing the recurrence of episodes for as long as possible.

We must persist in efforts to improve bipolar outcomes by continuing to examine the effectiveness of newer treatments for relapse prevention. Lithium has been viewed as the standard of care in maintenance treatment for people with bipolar disorder in the U.S. since 1971. However, in the past decade, anticonvulsants and, recently, atypical antipsychotics have improved as mood stabilizing medications that may assist in delaying relapse.

People with bipolar should be able to achieve the peace of mind and confidence to strive toward their personal goals without fear of relapsing. Hence they could deal with their disorder on a positive level.

It is my mission to promote awareness of bipolar disorder and discover all avenues of attaining total episode free emotional stability, by exploring the causes of relapse and educating people with bipolar disorder about how to delay and work toward prevention.

When I was instructed by my psychiatrist to stay on Lithium for the rest of my life, (He was a very strong minded Doc and did not pull any punches with me), I found myself fighting the concept of using Lithium indefinitely, so I came up with my own medical defense on the dangers of Lithium. I shared with him that we needed to evaluate tubular function and glomerular function in the kidney, and morphologic changes of glomerular and interstitial fibrosis and nephron atrophy had been reported in patients on chronic Lithium therapy.

He agreed wholeheartedly, clapping his hands, as he nodded in approval of my overly concerned dissertation. Leaning back in his chair, he looked me straight in the eyes, and said; "So, would you rather die from the possibility of glomerulitis or suicide?" He went on to say that the incidents of suicide, in my personal case, would be more problematic, than any kidney problems that may exist with Lithium. I had to reluctantly agree.

Now I have come "full circle" with the initial concern of how long term compliance with Lithium may affect my vital organs. And what are my choices: to continue with Lithium or risk my good record of stability?

Recently, my internist felt that because my creatinine levels in my kidneys was somewhat high at 2.20 (reference level .076 - 1.27), that the causative factor could be the longstanding usage of Lithium. For the past 27 years my Lithium levels have maintained a therapeutic level of 0.6 to 0.8 with a constant dose of 300 mg twice a day. However, my recent Lithium levels were creeping toward a toxic level of 1.5. So, my internist and I agreed to cut the Lithium dosage level in half or 150 mg twice a day. Being of my positive nature, I was pleased when the results were reviewed at 1.6 for creatinine (still slightly high), but a much lower level of Lithium at 0.5. And equally important was that I maintained a positive and balanced level of stability for the over a 3 month period of a reduced dosage of Lithium. Also, all my thyroid tests were within normal limits.

Perhaps these physiological tests can relate to a constant positive mind, and its importance with a person with bipolar to always maintain a balanced and positive approach with their medical treatment as well as their medications. If you can do that, and live that way, you are really a wise person. We can be sure that the greatest hope for maintaining equilibrium in the face of any situation rests within ourselves. I have learned that you cannot have everything and do everything at the same time.

Chapter 10:

Learning Awareness

Q...In what ways have you found that developing a stronger foundation with controlling your mind, body and emotions have helped you with potential mood swings?

A...Just learning "Awareness" of our emotions will give a bipolar a positive start to build the patience needed to off set the biochemical change within the brain.

Leonardo da Vinci suggests that patience serves as a protection against wrongs as clothes do against cold. If you put on more clothes as the cold increases, it will have no power to hurt you. So, in like manner you must grow in patience when you meet with great wrongs, and they will then be powerless to distress your mind. And lastly listen to Saint Francis de

Sales: Have patience with all things, but chiefly have patience with yourself. Do not lose courage in considering your own imperfections but instantly set about remedying them - every day begins the task anew.

Someone once said that bipolar disorder is a "Mind Game" that includes how our bodies work, how they heal, and all the various obstacles that represent the blockage we must overcome to get our lives back on the right track. The closer you are to your "Awareness", the better equipped you are to deal with what life throws at you, the more tightly connected you remain to your "Awareness," the more able you are to weather those storms of bipolar disorder. It is not always about getting it right again. It is all in the mental game and can only be won with exercising that muscle that brings "Awareness" into authority over the mind, body, and emotions. In many respects, bipolar disorder can be overcome with a concerted effort that applies the mind to the task of creating change, says P. Leedman, Australian medical researcher. The problem for most is they feel overwhelmed by and completely identify with whatever condition has been applied to their particular problem. Does this mean you have been diagnosed incorrectly? Not necessarily. It means you have more power over creating change than you might otherwise believe.

Understanding the cause and effect from "triggers", it is possible to realize the occurrence they have on bipolar disorder. Instead of simply treating the symptoms, anyone suffering also wants to treat the cause, to get to the root, to find the missing link and solve the outcome of the current experience they are living. How is it possible?

The main thing to recognize is your experience of self. Consider the mind and all its thoughts and all that thinking. What's going on with that and are you identifying yourself with those thoughts? I think most people are so naturally accustomed to the mind through the years of schooling, that when the negative spark that triggers a direction down an unhealthy path, the creeping in of that negative experience and those thoughts goes unnoticed, until it is too late to nip it in the bud. Now more intentional effort has to be applied to overcome what has built up over a period of time.

Now that brings us to emotions. We do feel things. Ironically, we rarely realize that emotions can be unreliable, even though they can be quite wonderful at times. These emotions often times are actually creations of the mind. Events happen that make us happy. Why do they make us happy? Usually, it relates to who we are, what we value and what we believe to be true, not to mention that we are so good at imagining positive outcomes that we desire in any moment that a wonderful emotion is triggered. Again, these emotions are most often triggered by the mind; they also carry chemicals that create physical feelings that reinforce emotions which in turn reinforce thought.

This brings us to the body. As emotions are expressions of feeling, the body also carries feelings that actually have little to do with emotion. There are discomfort, pain, and quite honestly, a whole plethora of physical sensations. What is important to realize is that the physical body can speak to you more frankly and honestly than both the mind and emotions.

You are the real you. When suffering from anything - mental, physical, or emotional - we become absorbed by that state of being. However, the mind sometimes barks at the situation - all the self-talk we are familiar with - expressing its frustration at this current reality. The mind remembers the good, the bad and the ugly, but mostly compares. Why am I like this now, when I was amazing before? It knows, and shows, the emotion kicks in as frustration begs for release and freedom from this painful reality. Sounds familiar of bipolar disorder?

When all the storms of your condition overwhelm you, have you ever noticed another aspect of yourself? It just sits there, another voice that speaks silently in awe, wonder, sadness, love, or curiosity and surrenders to your choice. However, when we are quiet with it, we recognize that it simply is "aware".

This awareness recognizes what is happening with the body, emotions, and thoughts, but has to wait for you to connect to your awareness before it can start bringing about change. Awareness also knows it is a process. It is in a physical world of natural law, and that nature's laws have cause-and-effect creating courses in our lives, and it knows that with nature's laws we are all subject to the processes of nature.

With understanding how our mind, body and emotions work together, we can look at pain. We may be learning to get the "pain's message." Peter Williams tells us that pain (any pain-emotional, physical, or mental) has a message. The information it has about our life can be remarkably specific, but it usually falls into one of two categories: "We would be more alive if we did more of this," and, "Life would be lovelier if we did less of that." Once we get the "pains message", and follow its advice, the pain goes away. A wise man should consider that health is the greatest of human blessings, and learn how by his own thought to derive benefit from his illnesses. Look to your health; if you have it, praise God and value it next to conscience; for health is the second blessing that we mortals are capable of, blessing money cannot buy.

Perhaps, this is what a person with bipolar disorder needs to hear when it is imperative to "push the positive." Thinking positive thoughts with the help of CBT Cognitive Behavioral Therapy will improve and aid the bipolar so he/she can manage their mood swings with an increased confidence.

Now try to visualize the Bipolar Stability Equation no one tells you about. May I suggest to you it is a little known concept? It comes from math, but the bottom line is, it is the content that is important. I am going to suggest to you a secret that very few people know. This is a secret to helping people with bipolar disorder stay stable. Stability is like a mathematical equation. Here are some of the things that can make up the equation. By using the KISS method (Keep It Simple Stupid):

• Medication
• Therapy
• Sleep
• Eating right
• Exercise
• Reducing stress/low anxiety
• The right job (or disability)
• A good support system
• Hobbies
• Relaxation/Meditation
• Watching for triggers

Everyone has to figure out what their own stability equation is: everyone is different (so their own stability equation is going to be different). One person may be able to keep their job, while another person may have to go on disability. One person may be a morning person, while another person may go to bed at midnight every night.

The things listed above are only examples of what may be in your stability equation. Other examples are light therapy, reading, watching a video, sitting watching a sunset, walking on the beach/taking long walks. We can consider the use of aromatherapy, homeopathy, acupuncture and biofeedback, etc.

The point is, you will have to make your own list and work with your doctor and therapist. One particular thing about people with bipolar disorder is that they need structure and routine to maintain stability. Watch out for your known episode triggers then try avoiding these triggers. Remember, you have to work hard to figure out the equation, and what to do if something goes wrong in the equation.

With knowing the foundation of the above equation, we can now build some "mind muscle" with what Medha Godbole labels as exercises for positive thinking. They say that your thoughts govern your words, which reach the brain and then the brain converts those into action. Hence first things first: we have to guide our thoughts toward something positive. If they are tending toward depression and negativity, that will have an impact on how your behavior is going to be. Visualize a positive image, think about things that make you happy, and try and keep the negativity in check.

Word Wise: As mentioned earlier, just as our words are a result of our thoughts, words also sometimes impact our thoughts. It is necessary therefore that we induce minimum negativity in our words. Always try and use positive words while talking. Never say 'I can't'. Just believe that you can or you will try your best. How will you know unless you push yourself? Constantly say things to your self like, 'I can', 'I will', I believe in myself'. Another aspect is to play around with words that make you happy and in still confidence in you. Make sure that the words you use evoke power and a sense of achievement. These are a major part of your positive self-affirmation. Belief is the key: if you just mutter these affirmations to yourself just for the sake of doing so, it would be futile. For these affirmations to work, you have to believe in yourself. Have faith in yourself that you will succeed. You will get what you want. Better still, just believe that you are there and bang! Try this as it is one of the 'best sellers' amongst positive thinking exercises.

-Gratitude, the best policy: Okay, you gripe about what went wrong. For a change, thank your stars or the supernatural powers of God or anything you believe in for what you have. Start being grateful for all the good things you have and then see the difference. Begin your day with a big thank you for a wonderful day to come in advance. This is a very effective method to infuse positive thinking in our lives:

-Make a list: List all the things you want in your life and visualize how you are going to get them. Be positive about the fact that you are going to get those things. Justify to yourself why you deserve these things and why you are going to get these things. Focus on the reasons for getting them, instead of why you might not get them. This is one of those positive thinking techniques which is sure to help you in the long run.

-The flip side: They say that every coin has two sides. Each situation of our life is also like that. It is just that sometimes we only perceive one side. Of course unfortunate things happen to us. But try and see what could have happened and what has been a positive outcome of that unfortunate incident. See the good part, as every cloud has a silver lining.

-Happy days: Indulge in a thing, every day, which makes you happy and forget about all the worldly worries and tensions of mere mortals. It could be hitting the gym, going to a dance or music class, listening to music, reading a book, cooking or anything under the sun. It should of course be apart from your work. Once the relaxing effect of these activities trickles down, you will get into that positive mode. This is one of the easiest and must-do positive thinking tips.

Researchers bring to consumers break-through science and as they discover the intricacies of the human brain as they move revolutionarily forward. Today, patients are treated differently, with medications that help greatly, and though we battle the stigma of bipolar disorder (I, II, III, and IV), we are ahead of the game. When we understand the clinical picture obtained from the technology age of ours, we can see clearly how the pieces come together to complete the puzzle.

Chapter 11:

Positive Inspirations from Authors and Philosophers

Q...Can you give us some examples of how well-know authors and celebrities who kindled your attitude and promoted an increase in your positive thinking with bipolar disorder?

Edith Wharton tells us there are lots of ways of being miserable, but there is only one way of being comfortable, and that is to stop running around after happiness. If you make up your mind to be happy there is no reason why you should not have a fairly good time.
Perhaps that is all a bipolar needs to do is "make up your mind." It is the willingness to be positive about all our moods that will bring about happiness and then stability.

Eddie Cantor, a loveable comedian from

years past, says that happiness always brings humor and laughter. If there were in the world today, any large number of people who desired their own happiness more than they desired the unhappiness of others, we could have paradise in a few years.

And Bertrand Russell encourages us to slow down and enjoy life. It is not only the scenery you miss by going too fast, you also miss the sense of where you are going and why.

Mark Twain reminds us that humor is the great thing, the saving thing. The minute it crops up, all our irritations and resentment slip away and a sunny spirit takes place.

Ralph Marston, from the *Daily Motivator* provides comments about the importance of positive thinking. He states: "If you have gotten off to a slow start, now is your opportunity to speed up. If you've been disappointed by the results so far, now is the chance to make some effective positive changes.

"Negative momentum can be powerful. Yet, the moment you commit yourself to a positive perspective, that negative momentum is gone. Perhaps you could stop worrying and complaining about the fact that your day, your week, your month or your life has gotten off to a bad start. Use this moment right now to interrupt the pattern and point yourself in a positive, empowered, fulfilling direction.

"Your past has brought you where you are, and yet it does not dictate where you can now go. Make the choice to point all of your life in the direction of your dreams.

"Even though you may have experienced great difficulty in getting started, choose now to be thankful for those difficulties you have gone through. Be thankful for the strength they have enabled you to build, and make positive use of that strength going forward.

"This time, this moment is different, because now you're in complete control and determined to make it great. So no matter what may have happened, get over it, and get going toward the best you can imagine."

Marston goes on to say, "though there's much you can do, there's nothing you must do to make yourself more important. You're already extremely important.

"You are already unique, valuable, and worthy. For you are expressions of life like no other.

"You are life experiencing the beauty and miracle of itself, blissfully and powerfully aware of your own awareness. Nothing you strive for or fight over could be more monumental than that.

"You long to create beautiful moments, and your ambitions can indeed bring much new beauty into existence. Always keep in mind, though, that you already have an exquisitely beautiful moment, and it is here, now.

"There is plenty of space and opportunity for real meaning and fulfillment right now, where you are. Instead of hurrying on to something you perceive as being more, feel the fullness of joy that is already a part of you.

"Bring all the power of the sweet experiences you fondly recall, and the future joy you wish to create, into making new, fulfilling meaning in this moment right now. The here and now is where you belong, and where you can always be your very best."

Karen Raven adds this: "Only as high as I reach can I grow; only as far as I seek can I go; only as deep as I look can I see: only as much as I dream can I be."

I find that this is one of the most positive statements any person living with bipolar disorder can ultimately achieve. I try to look at this quote at the start of each day. However, I ask myself, why did I choose this quote? What meanings does it hold for me, now that I have aged? So, I decided to find some meaning into these phrases. With a little help from other quotes, I found an answer:

-Only has high as I reach can I grow..."Anyone can give up; it is the easiest thing in the world to do. But to hold it together when everyone else would understand if you fell apart, that's true strength" Author unknown.

-Only as far as I seek can I go..."When it is obvious that the goals cannot be reached, do not adjust the goals, and adjust the action steps" Confucius.

-Only as deep as I look can I see..."Courage does not always roar. Sometimes courage is too deep inside and is difficult to see or hear the quiet voice at the end of the day saying, 'I will try again tomorrow' Mary Anne Radmacher.

-Only as much as I dream can I be..."If your actions inspire others to dream more, learn more, do more and become more, then they will lead to leadership" John Quincy Adams.

Don Miguel Ruiz suggests "Four Agreements" that are extremely useful for people with bipolar disorder for staying positive and optimistic.

-1) Be Impeccable with Your Words: Speak with integrity. Say only what you mean. Avoid using the word to speak against yourself or to gossip about others. Use the power of your words in the direction of truth and love.

-2) Do not Take Anything Personally: Nothing others do is because of you. What others say and do is a projection of their own reality, their own dream. When you are immune to the opinions and actions of others, you won't be the victim of needless suffering.

3) Do not Make Assumptions: Find the courage to ask questions and to express what you really want. Communicate with

others as clearly as you can to avoid misunderstandings, sadness, and drama. With just this one agreement, you can completely transform your life.

-4) Always Do Your Best: Your best is going to change from moment to moment; it will be different when you are healthy as opposed to sick. Under any circumstance, simply do your best and you will avoid self-judgment, self-abuse, and regret.

Dr. Wayne Dyer writes in his book, *Change Your Thoughts – Change Your Life*, about "The Calm Center." Perhaps, this may be one of the most positive foundations for living with bipolar disorder:

"Seek a calm inner response to the circumstances of your life. In the midst of any kind of unrest--be it an argument, school pressures, a traffic jam, a monetary crisis, parental pressures, or anything at all--make the immediate decision that you will find the "Calm Center" of yourself. By not thinking of what is taking place, and instead taking a few deep breaths in which you opt to employ your mind of judgments; it becomes impossible to mentally "flit about like a fool". Work toward having the innate ability to choose "Calmness" in the face of situations that may drive you to mood changes. Your willingness to do so, especially when chaos and anger have been your previous choices, puts you in touch with 'Calmness'."

There was a time when I thought this was impossible, now I know even in the most troublesome of times, my reaction to choose
Stillness will produce "Calmness".

If we can achieve "Calmness" then we will find that controlling anger may come easier.

Brian Adams teaches us the art of patience. "Apply discipline to your thoughts when they become anxious over the outcome of a goal. Impatience breeds anxiety, fear, discouragement and failure. Patience creates confidence, decisiveness and a rational outlook, which eventually leads to success. I have learned silence from the talkative, toleration from the intolerant, and kindness from the unkind. Though strange, I am ungrateful to these teachers."

So, as I study to understand patience and tolerance, it leads me to conquer and override anger. Can I put these two characteristics, patience and tolerance, into practice every time I am exposed to anger? I am trying...it seems to be working.

We can build on our patience by developing self-confidence and learning to look at the positive thinking from these quotes from Anna Freud, Andre Gode and Norman Vincent Peale :

"I was always looking outside myself for strength and confidence, but it comes from within. It is there all the time."

"There are admirable potentialities in every human being. Believe in your strength and your youth. Learn to repeat endlessly to yourself: it all depends on me."

Having once decided to achieve a certain task, achieve it at all costs of tedium and distaste. The gain in self-confidence of having accomplished a tiresome labor is immense."

Gordon Atkinson emphasizes forgiveness does not always lead to a healed relationship. Some people are not capable of love, and it might be wise to let them go along with their anger. Wish

them well, and let them go their way.
Forgiveness is the healing of wounds
caused by another. You choose to let go
of a past wrong and no longer be hurt by
it. Forgiveness is a strong move to make,
like turning your shoulders sideways to
walk quickly on a crowded sidewalk. It is
your move. It really does not matter if
the person who hurt you deserves to be
forgiven. Forgiveness is a gift you give
yourself. You have things to do and you
want to move on.

Mitch Albom's book, *Have a Little Faith*,
has caused me to ponder some very
important aspects for bipolar challenges,
with faith, in our everyday lives:

1). Have a little faith in yourself. You can
search throughout the entire universe for
someone who is more deserving of your
love and affection than you are yourself;
that person is not to be found anywhere.
You, yourself, as much as anybody in the
entire universe deserve your love and
affection. Remind yourself daily that you
can overcome a negative feeling or
mood.

2). Have a little faith in your psychiatrist.
In general, most psychiatrists will
suggest the truth is, that our finest
moments are most likely to occur when

we are feeling deeply uncomfortable, unhappy, or unfulfilled. For it is only in such moments, propelled by our discomfort, that we are likely to step out of our ruts and start searching for different ways or truer answers. It is then we must be willing to fail and to appreciate the truth that often life is not a problem to be solved, but a mystery to be lived.

3). Have a little faith in your medications. Perhaps the smartest thing for people to do to manage very distressing emotions is to take a medication if it helps, but not only that; you also need to train your mind and educate yourself about the medications and always be compliant. You then will receive stability from it. Remember, if it keeps you stable, do not think you do not need to take it anymore.

4). Have a little faith in the side effects. Laughter is a tranquilizer with no side effects. Remember, most side effects will diminish within three weeks if the medication is right for you. If the side effects are still a problem then the dosage may be the cause. By the reduction of side effects, your stability will be enhanced and the medication will prove adequate for you.

5). Have a little faith in your moods. Prepare yourself to be positive about a mood shift. Do not wait for moods. You accomplish nothing if you do that. Your mind must know it needs to work. The heart loves, but moods have no loyalty. Moods should be heard but never danced to. Faith is the art of holding on to things your reason once accepted, despite your changing moods.

6). Believe in yourself! Have faith in your abilities! Without a humble but reasonable confidence in your own powers, you cannot be successful or happy.

By learning and developing these methods of faith, we then can start with positive decision-making. Making decisions can always produce positive action for all people with bipolar disorder.

-"I think that somehow, we learn who we really are and then live with that decision. It is our choices that show what we truly are, far more than our abilities." Eleanor Roosevelt.

-"The self is not something ready-made, but something in continuous formation through choice of action." John Dewey.

-"If you limit your choices only to what seems possible or reasonable, you disconnect yourself from what you truly want, and all that is left is a compromise." Robert Fritz.

-"Men acquire a particular quality by constantly acting a particular way...you become just by performing just actions, temperate by performing temperate actions, brave by performing brave actions." Aristotle.

-"I have long since come to believe that people never mean half of what they say, and that it is best to disregard their talk and judge only their actions." Dorothy Day.

-"Don't be too timid and squeamish about your actions. All life is an experiment. The more experiments you make, the better." -Ralph Waldo Emerson.

Working toward kindness will bring joy to the bipolar that needs to overcome daily symptoms and to stay positive with stability. It has been said that creativity is the bipolar's gift to all mankind. However, in order to keep creativity positive, and productive, listen to the words from the following:

"The problem is never how to get new, innovative thoughts into your mind, but how to get old ones out. Every mind is a building filled with archaic furniture. Clean out a corner of your mind and creativity will instantly fill it." Dee Hock.

"The creation of something new is not accomplished by the intellect but by the play instinct acting from inner necessity. The creative mind plays with the objects it loves." Carl Jung.

"Creativity is seeing something that doesn't exist already. You need to find out how you can bring it into being and that way be a playmate with God." Michele Shea.

"Creativity can solve almost any problem. The creative act, the defeat of habit by originality, overcomes everything." George Lois.

"The ideals which have lit my way and time after time have given me new courage to face life cheerfully, have been kindness, beauty and truth. The trite subjects of human efforts, possessions, outward success, and luxury have always seemed to me contemptible." Albert Einstein.

"Guard well within yourself that treasure, kindness. Know how to give without hesitation, how to lose without regret, how to acquire without meanness" George Sands.

"This is the true joy in life, the being used for a purpose recognized by yourself as a mighty one; the being thoroughly worn out before you are thrown on the scrap heap; the being a force of Nature instead of a feverish selfish little clod of ailments and grievances complaining that the world will not devote itself to making you happy." George Bernard Shaw.

"Give not over thy soul to sorrow; and afflict not thyself in thy own counsel. Gladness of heart is the life of man and the joyfulness of man is length of days." Ecclesiastes.

"I cannot believe that the inscrutable universe turns on an axis of suffering; surely the strange beauty of the world must somewhere rest on pure joy!" Louis Bogan.

You may remember the "creative" scene

in Woody Allen's "Annie Hall" where Woody tells the story of the man who goes to the psychiatrist, complaining that his brother-in-law, who lives with him, thinks he is a chicken.

"Describe his symptoms," the doctor says, "and maybe I can help."

The man replies, "Well, he cackles a lot, he pecks at the rug and the furniture and he makes nests in the corners."

The doctor thinks for a moment, and then says, "It sounds like a simple neurosis to me. Bring your brother-in-law in and I think I can cure him completely."

"Oh no, Doc," says the man, "we wouldn't want that! We need the eggs."

Even when we are captured by destructive neuroses we are still, curiously, unwilling to change. Even when life becomes sick and destructive it is better, we convince ourselves, than the unknown. So much of bipolar disorder seems to be centered on this reluctance to change. We cling desperately to the past. We cling because it has worked for us then, so why not now?

Your past thoughts are about events that are no longer real. That bad experience happened yesterday (in the past) and is over. It is gone and exists solely in your mind. Today is a new day, a better day, and worrying about the past just dooms us in the present. It is how you process it now that makes a difference.

Chapter 12:

Learning the Art of Self-Help

Q...What would be other positive suggestions, Dr. Fred, which you have found to continue your healthy mental habits and controlling not only your physical needs, but your psychological needs to maintain stability? Have you found that "Self-help" is a practical means to controlling and overcoming bipolar disorder?

A...Perhaps, we all have a secret need to find that natural cure for bipolar disorder. In the last 28 years, I have read, studied and researched a multitude of information looking for the answer. Oddly enough I found it just looking at my "Self". One of my resources came from this concept of "Self-help":

We all know it is possible to treat and manage bipolar disorder with proper medications that lead to a positive level of stability. I can emphatically say that my success with Lithium has given me my long term stability, and I could not have achieved it without my complete compliance. Although you might be taking medication to deal with your bipolar disorder right now, "bipolar self-help" is a necessary tool to help manage your success; toward achieving a maximum balance and long term stability with bipolar disorder.

Antidepressant and psychiatric care or therapy have their place, but currently there is not enough emphasis being placed on the power of practicing 'self-help' for those who need an adjunct stimulus to help manage bipolar disorder.

The most essential element of exercising 'self help' is becoming acutely conscious of your thinking. The worst episodes always begin with small, seemingly harmless thoughts. Small thoughts in turn grow into something increasingly irrational, and soon another explosive episode is born.

Learning to control and master your thinking is an intensive process that requires tremendous self-discipline and deep awareness of your personal tendencies. To achieve freedom from bipolar disorder, it is necessary to comply with proper medications, and only then it may be possible once you find the key to making fundamental changes in your mood patterns and thinking.

Perhaps the biggest tragedy of being afflicted by bipolar disorder is the frequent inability to create healthy situations and prevent destructive ones. In struggling against the disorder, those afflicted often bring about horrific pain, tumult and heartache. One must exert control over the small thoughts that initially lead to irrational and poisonous emotions. Therefore, it is necessary to master the thoughts that precede this eventual commitment. When struggling to maintain a healthy mood and rational thinking, you can simply declare within that you have firmly committed to not letting an episode flare up. You must then become unambiguously dedicated to a beneficial, non-explosive, neutral or even positive outcome.

The underlying thinking here is that you are converting what potentially began as something destructive and toxic, into what has the possibility of being a normal, safe, and advantageous result. By working with a positive self-help attitude in conjunction with your medications, this will act as a powerful affirmation that you can continue to build a strong sense of stability. You are in control of your thinking, your moods, and your life. Believing you have control over yourself is absolutely imperative to positively affecting your reality. When supported by your medications, you have a positive chance of effectively thwarting potential episodes.

When feeling the onset of mania, the opportunity for performing a highly effective self-help test becomes crucially important. This consists of taking a step back from where you currently are emotionally and psychologically and evaluating the antithesis of your feelings. Therefore if you feel angry that your husband didn't clean the kitchen, imagine what it would be like to feel happy that your husband cleaned the kitchen. Although obviously not the case, and while you may indeed have valid reasons to be angry, the point with this exercise is to create massive contrast - the antithesis or opposite of what you are presently experiencing. For those who are capable of doing this, a fresh understanding of your own perspective is obtainable. It then becomes easier to resist letting the situation control you, and enables you to control your moods and thoughts irrespective of any current external factors. The main point here is that it doesn't matter if you are vindicated in feeling angry at the messy kitchen (or any other similar situation); you are choosing consciously to refuse to allow external circumstances to dictate the inner dispositions.

There is most certainly hope for living a normal life free of this disorder. In my case I feel, at the present time, Lithium is needed as an adjunct with the proper self-help techniques to reach the potential future goal of cure.

Q...Dr. Fred, do you feel that mastering this "self-help" concept has enabled you to be permanently cured?

A...Perhaps in the future with genetics advanced research this cure will be possible. I have achieved over 28 years of "episode free emotional stability" with bipolar disorder. Truly, the combination of Lithium compliance, monitoring my medication, self-help concepts, positive thinking and family/environmental support has provided years of episode free emotional stability.

Q...Therefore, Dr. Fred, do you believe that "episode free emotional stability" is possible?

A...I believe it is possible. However, the question is very difficult to answer for all mental health providers. Perhaps, I might suggest that a couple of years may be just a start of "episode free emotional stability." My psychiatrist has followed my episodes over a 25 year period before they began to stabilize. That was when we started to monitor my stability (1984). He stated that as long as a true episode cycle does not occur within a full year period, we could label that an "episode free emotionally stable" year...I visit my psychiatrist once a year for review of any possible episodes. This last visit I commented that I again, have not had a single episode...and now it has been 28 years without an episode. I suggested this..."So, possibly now I may be 'Functionally Cured'...He just smiled and said ...."Ah, but you are still a bipolar."

I try to promote the positive when it comes to answering the above question...It is very true that things do not heal you, others do not heal, only we can heal ourselves with the help of the medical profession.

An episode should include full blown mania and a resultant depression as a significant bipolar cycle. However, a very mild swing with "controlled" up (hypomania) and a mild down (depression) is always possible with bipolar II and is still considered an episode. Both bipolar 1 and bipolar II needs to know their triggers thoroughly and be able to call on all their "self-help" coping skills along with possible medication changes, when minor ups and downs occur so a full blown episode does not occur.

In my fight to control bipolar disorder it is imperative that you never lose hope, never give up, and actively seek out the information that provides lasting answers in order to develop a mastery of the "self."

Dealing with bipolar disorder is truly a challenge for many of us. Often times, I have wondered what is one of the basic traits that a person with bipolar needs. Perhaps, it could be "self development".

Did you ever wonder why many people go through the motions of life without ever knowing what potentialities they have and what heights they can scale if only they would make an organized effort and strive to transcend mediocrity? The chief purpose of all our education, whether it is science or humanities, and the central purpose of all our activities should be self-actualization through self-development In the end that alone would give us the satisfaction that we have lived our lives meaningfully. It is motivational and inspirational material that we need. It is all about self-development through sustained self-effort and efficient and intelligent utilization of available physical and mental resources. There are immense opportunities we all have if only we dare to be different and dare to be ourselves. Therein lies some of our answers to self-development with bipolar disorder.

Often times, my friends will share with me that they have never really gained full control over their self-esteem and self-confidence, even since their first diagnosis with bipolar disorder. I had the same anxieties to overcome.

I would like to share some "points" that were helpful for me a number of years ago. The greatest hope for maintaining equilibrium in the face of any situation rests within ourselves:

Self-esteem increases your self-confidence. If you have self-confidence you will respect yourself and then you can respect others, improve your relationships and become happier. This is not a selfish goal as you will contribute more and share yourself with the world and those around you.

1. Face your fears - challenges seem scary but your fears are usually exaggerated. Facing your fears increases your confidence and boosts your esteem. Dr. David M. Burns reminds us that "Fear always lurks behind perfectionism. Confronting your fears and allowing yourself the right to be human can, paradoxically, make you a far happier and more productive person."

2. Forget your failures - learn from them. Avoid making the same mistakes again but don't limit yourself by assuming you failed before so you cannot succeed this time. Try again, you are wiser and stronger. Do not be trapped in the past.

3. Know what you want and ask for it. Learn about being assertive. You deserve to have your dreams come true!

4. Reward yourself when you succeed.

No one else will! Is not everything easier when you take time to help yourself? Make a list of your successes and focus on the positive.

5. Talk - We often make assumptions about a situation or person which are not true. Your attitude and behavior can be negatively affected so if you have any doubt or question ask and don't assume you know why or how.

6. Don't be defeated! Try something else. You are not going to be defeated by one failed attempt are you? Does not everyone fail before they succeed? All you need is a different approach. Good luck! I wish you happiness and success!

7. It is amazing that self-hypnosis will build your self-esteem. I used this technique in my practice.

Now, the ball is in your corner If you ever played soccer you know that you cannot stand there and look at the ball.....just believe in your self....and kick the heck out of it ...you are going to make a goal!

There are a number of techniques to utilize self-confidence and self-esteem and put them into positive use. By

combining   self-hypnosis   with
visualization, one can achieve a true
sense of stress-reducing skills.

Visualization and self- hypnosis are two
techniques often used as part of a
holistic healing philosophy. Practitioners
of each believe the mind and body share
such a deep connection that treating one
should involve treating the other as well.
A number of historic and modern cultures
practice forms of visualization and self-
hypnosis, from the ancient Greeks, Sufis
and Egyptians to modern Tibetans and
Hindus.

Visualization is a form of relaxation
therapy in which you visualize comforting
images in an effort to relieve stress and
anxiety. Combining it with self-hypnosis,
you can immerse yourself in the image,
closing your eyes and letting all your
senses   absorb   the   details   your
imagination presents. There is not a one-
size-fits-all image for everyone---you
might visualize a person, a place, an
animal, an imaginary scene or anything
that gives you a sense of calm and well-
being. Visualization is often accompanied
by soothing music that complements
your image. The process is meant to be
relaxing and empowering at the same
time, giving you a way to tap into your

inner strength and channel your mental resources to regain a sense of balance. So, with these two techniques, a person with bipolar disorder may minimize their mood changes in a positive fashion.

I would like to suggest that "self-help" can be accomplished with the use of storytelling as it relates to psychology. Storytelling has been with us since the days of campfire and besieging wild animals. It served a number of important functions: amelioration of fears, communication of vital information (regarding survival tactics and the characteristics of animals, for instance) the satisfaction of a sense of order (justice), and the development of the ability to hypothesize, predict and introduce theories and so on. We are all endowed with a sense of wonder. The world around us is inexplicable; baffling in its diversity and myriad forms. We experience an urge to organize it, to "explain the wonder away", to order it so as to know what to expect next (predict). These are the essentials of survival. But while we have been successful at imposing our minds' structures on the outside world - we have been much less successful when we tried to cope with our internal universe. Is there a relationship between the structure and functioning of our (ephemeral) mind and the structure and modes of operation of our (physical) brain so that the two will merge with the structure and conduct of the outside world? Perhaps, our own "Self-Help" can use storytelling techniques in determining how we view our experiences and how they affect our lives in relationship to our personal understanding of how we fit into our own bipolar world. We can work through our troubled psyche and the distortions and learned behavior that we have!

I believe in the high functioning of people with bipolar disorder, especially if they have had effective medical care. My psychiatrist says that the longer people live with this illness, well-managed, the better their functioning becomes. He has told me that my functionality and stability has been the longest, at 28 years that he has ever experienced with any of his patients. When I compare what my life was like when I was in my twenties, thirties and forties, I can see that my life now - at 70 years old - is much easier to handle. And I, too, have achieved the same level of success as most of my non-bipolar friends - especially professionally and creatively.

Personally, I think that the bipolar can be

very functional if the person takes care of themselves properly. Unfortunately, there are the bipolar that are on medication, but they smoke, do drugs, drink, and just don't take care of themselves. They may even use their bipolar as an excuse for their bad habits. Being on Lithium, I have maintained functionality and stability, and have been creative and very productive; even in my retirement years.

I have my moments of wanting to paint the town red so to speak, but I stop myself of course. For me, at least, Lithium allows me to stay cool and in control. Because the bipolar can cope with life's demands as well as any other person, it would be great if society realized this...Perhaps, then the stigma would die down.

Because, high functionality and creativeness come with bipolar, it is up to the person to use it effectively. As for the stigma, I do not think it will go away altogether in society. People with bipolar can make it go away in their own social environments and amongst people around them. In my experience, I think medication is a helping hand in the times of need, but what we make of ourselves is much more important. Learning to use

Self-Help is the answer.

Chapter 13:

Breaking the Fears of Bipolar Disorder

Q...What have you learned about fear as it relates to the causes and precipitation of bipolar episodes?

A...Breaking the cycle of fear is the "simple" answer to allow a person to never fear another panic attack, or a bipolar mood episode.

The major thing that has people searching for a solution to anxiety/ panic attacks or mood disorders is the fear of having another one. When this happens, people begin to either avoid situations that make them anxious or they self-medicate themselves to the point where they are numb to the fear. I am sure you will agree, neither of the above is a satisfactory solution. We need to give people the ability to immediately stop fearing another panic attack and/or mood disorder. It is very simple, yet amazingly effective. What seems to happen is a mental imprint generates a cycle or loop of anxiety whereby the person develops an unhealthy fear of having another panic attack or mood disorder. What is simply needed is to allow that person to break the cycle of anxiety and return to normal everyday living. There is no need to regress into the past and find out why an initial panic attack occurred. All that is needed is the simple willingness to break out of the cycle of fear.

Dune's *Litany against Fear* has a different take on fear. He emphasizes that we must not fear. Fear is the mind-killer. Fear is the little death that brings total obliteration. We will face our fears. We will permit it to pass over us and through us. When it has gone past we will turn our inner Third Eye (The Pineal Gland) to see its path. Where the fear has gone there will be nothing. Only we will remain.

Everyone has experienced feeling afraid of something. Fear has a legitimate function since it alerts us to something that could possibly be harmful. Usually, we are able to assess the situation and see if there is any real danger, then take steps to deal with the problem. However, sometimes our fear interferes with the activities of daily living. We may have a restless sleep, difficulty concentrating or loss of appetite. This is often frustrating because we think of our fear as unrealistic but remain hampered by it.

Management of the emotional impact of fear takes time and involves different feelings. While we know there is a wide range of common, normal reactions to experiences of fear, we also know that each person may not have exactly the same feelings or reactions. Sometimes feelings can change quickly or seem to go from one extreme to another. Try to be understanding of yourself and those you care about, and recall that you may not have the same feelings, or have them at exactly the same time. Reactions may be cognitive, physical, behavioral or emotional. Fear reduction takes time, but will take place when you provide adequate self-care, and elicit support.

I have come to realize that my family is the most important part of my life. It requires an open mind, but foremost a change of attitude that may lie at the bottom of an unconscious fear. For now is a time to look back and learn to be mellow. Our deepest fear is not that we are inadequate. Our deepest fear is that we are powerful beyond measure. It is our light, not our darkness, which frightens us most. We ask ourselves, 'Who am I to be brilliant, gorgeous, talented, and famous?' Actually, who are you not to be? Your playing small does not serve the world. There is nothing enlightened about shrinking so that people won't feel insecure around you. We were born to make manifest the glory of God that is within us. It's not just in some of us; it's in all of us. And when we let our own light shine, we unconsciously give other people permission to do the same. As we are liberated from our own fear, our presence automatically liberates others.

Insomniac, (it rhymes with maniac)...and that is what those of us cursed by this particular nocturnal affliction fear we'll become. Drive around the neighborhood some night around 2:00 a.m. and note whose windows are illuminated. The fear of insomnia is insidious. Inside these windows, you would more than likely discover one more fellow sufferer pacing the living room floor, gazing vacantly at the television screen, reading the latest

Grisham pot-boiler or just lying in bed listening to the strange sounds a house makes only in the middle of the night. They say insomnia is the result of a guilty conscience which only makes those of us who cannot sleep stay up later wondering what we are guilty of. But the truth is that the insomniac is avoiding his own fears, the fear of confronting his bipolar. Making matters worse, the most important element of a healthy lifestyle is a good night's sleep. Do you have any idea what effect that kind of judgment has on the poor soul whose eyes refuse to close and mind resists shutting down? It actually just provides one more reason for staying awake. We need to analyze, investigate, examine, study, explore, research and review the evidence from every angle imaginable before even considering turning off the light. Of course, when all that is done, a paradox continues, we will once again discover that although we are now well versed on the issue, we are too tense to drop off. Perhaps, "self-help" could be one of the best tools we could ever use with insomnia. We are the best source of our own nightly patterns. Confronting our mood changes and acknowledging the reasons for them to occur, we may be able find that positive return to a good night's sleep.

Don't be discouraged by fear of failure. It can be a positive experience. By reducing the fear, failure is, in a sense, the highway to success, inasmuch as every discovery of what is false leads us to seek earnestly after what is true. Every fresh experience points out some form of error which we shall afterwards carefully avoid. If you have made mistakes, even serious ones, there is always another chance for you. What we call failure is not the falling down but the staying down. I cannot give you a sure-fire formula for success, but I can give you a formula for failure; trying to please everybody all the time. Perhaps, it is the underlying fear of life's failures that cause people to give up, when they did not realize how close they were to success. To use fear as the friend it is, we must retrain and reprogram ourselves...We must persistently and convincingly tell ourselves that the fear is here--with its gift of energy and heightened awareness--so we can do our best and learn the most in the new situation.

Fear may be a possible basis for a disorder. It is therefore, a good reason to look fear in the face and start to believe in ourselves in the utmost positive ways.

"Fear is a question: What are you afraid of, and why? Just as the seeds of health are in illness, because illness contains information, your fears are a treasure house of self- knowledge if you explore them." Marilyn Ferguson.

As a young boy, I was plagued with the fear of bipolar disorder. I remember exciting adventures and new discoveries. At times, life was filled with fears of depression. And yet, there were some times filled with great pleasure, but always there was an underlying fear. By then I had a pretty good idea of what my folks knew, but still there was one surprise after another. Some were painful revelations of watching my father trying to deal with his bipolar. I suppose I respected their advice and honored their counsel, but still I wanted to seek reasons for this fear that haunted me. I needed this for myself and to not just go through it vicariously. Frightened at times, confused at others, I grieved that I might be missing out on the great adventures of life, of exploring what to believe and why to believe it, of discovering the marvel of the mind and the miracles that can come when using it. Perhaps, it was this underlying fear that forced my mind to find better choices, to discover that I could overcome what I saw in my parents' lives and move forward with a positive attitude of the pending bipolar disorder that would eventually consume my life. With time, patience, proper guidance, and medication I found the precursors to overcoming my fear of bipolar disorder. And I am still experiencing a whole new stable life of discovery.

Perhaps, Eleanor Roosevelt gives we who are bipolar, the ultimate suggestion in controlling fear: "You gain strength, courage and confidence by every experience in which you really stop to look fear in the face. You are able to say to yourself, 'I have lived through this horror. I can take the next thing that comes along.' You must do the things you think you cannot do."

In men of the highest character and noblest genius there is to be found an insatiable desire for honor, command, power, glory and the gift of controlling fear.

Chapter 14:

Character Building Techniques

Q...There are so many methods you have shared with us to continually keep bipolar in a positive vein. What have you found complements your attitude and are there techniques that you and others can use to continue to give encouragement?

A...How do you harness the power of bipolar? First, you learn as much as you can about it. Second, you build in daily reality checks. Third, you embrace this so-called disorder. Learn to appreciate your heightened state of sensitivity. If you have bipolar, you may already be familiar with the highs of being manic. Your moods will fluctuate, so the key is to recall the strength you feel from such a high and use it to your best advantage when you are mentally stable, and to recall that same strength when you are feeling the lows of bipolar. Try to maintain a sense of normalcy while celebrating that you are different. Enjoy your uniqueness and the fact that you were born different than most for a God given reason. At the same time, learn to see the signs of manic behavior because you will probably burn out at some point from being manic for any length of time. Don't allow yourself to sink deep into the bellows of depression because it is hard to get out of a depressed state.

Think of the many times a day that negativity arises. You are cut off in traffic and a little light goes off in the back of your brain. You seethe and seek to retaliate, your blood pressure rises, and your heart beats faster. This is not what the doctor recommends when he says give your heart some exercise! Wouldn't it be wonderful if such disruptions never occurred? It can happen, of course. It is entirely up to us. We decide if violence and anger will control us, or peace and love. No one has to describe the benefits of living a life of peace over one of war. It is the same on the battlefields of the world and in the battlefield of our own soul. It is just that we must always fight for a positive view point, if we're caught in that vicious cycle of bipolar disorder.

Chance is always powerful. Let your hook be always cast in the pool where you least expect it. Ovid says, "Here will be a fish."(But, I would rather have the "choice"). Williams Jennings Bryan suggests destiny is no matter of chance. It is a matter of choice. It is not a thing to be waited for. It is a thing to be achieved. It's choice - not chance - that determines your destiny.

Ramana Maharshi states there is no greater mystery than this, that we keep seeking reality though in fact we are reality. We think that there is something hiding reality and that this must be destroyed before reality is gained. How ridiculous! A day will dawn when you will laugh at all your past efforts. That which will be the day you laugh is also here and now. However, I agree with Michelle Miller-Lallow with her thoughts that in the essence of life, the reality is that we do not live in days, hours, and minutes of time. That is our perception now. As we realize our reality, we become one with it and it with us so there is no separation or distinction only reality. The day of enlightenment is the day we accept that reality.

-The Power of Acceptance:
I suspect some of us need heroes and

heroines. In a world filled with ambiguity, it is very tempting to create super humans who will fool us into thinking that the answers of life really are simple and plain. I cannot tell you how many times I have sat and listened as someone struggling with the problems of life spoke of their desire to be like someone else. "If only my life was like Bill or Mary so-and-so." What they don't realize or don't want to acknowledge, of course, is that Bill and Mary have their own set of problems and may even have expressed their desire to be like someone else, as well. The trick is not to try and be like someone else but to discover ways of accepting who we are. For the bipolar, this concept of learning to develop goals toward stability is extremely important. Finding ways to cope and deal with mood swings cannot be denied. Remember, bipolar disorder does not define a person. Working toward the understanding of controlling our own actions toward ourselves and others is ultimately the answer for the bipolar to choose.

-The Power of Forgiveness:
Perhaps, as we grow with our own bipolar disorder, we can approach the positive forgiveness that is needed to gain stability. From what I witness, over

and over again, I discover how satisfying living for others can be. The folks whose lives have meaning and purpose, who have a real zest for living, spend little of their time worried about themselves and a great deal of time giving to others.

Elisha Goldstein suggests "we all hold grudges against other people who we feel have hurt or offended us in some way or another. We even hold these grudges for people who are not even alive anymore. We do this with the false idea that somehow we are making them suffer by being hurt and angry with them."

As for me, I've seen enough unforgiving to be utterly convinced that it is about as destructive a thing as there can be. There is a kind of peace that is clearly observable among people who have the courage to forgive others and themselves. I like being around those folks. I'll bet you do too.

-The Power of Honesty:
What a terrible place to be when all of society prescribes anything but honesty. Be cool. Be in control. Be anything but open. Find something, anything, to cover up, to hide the naked truth. Surely one of the greatest failures of mankind is our

unwillingness to be open and honest with either God or each other. So much of our life is based on pretense, on lies. We dare not confess our need for each other. We dare not cry out our despair or our doubting for fear that others will think we don't have it all together. One of the greatest therapeutic discoveries of this century has been the realization that the best source of emotional healing is found not with the experts but with the experienced. Alcoholics Anonymous, NAMI, bipolar support groups, cancer support groups, divorce recovery organizations, these are the places where real healing is taking place. It is not coincidental that these are the places of honesty, openness and vulnerability. These are Gardens of Eden and should serve as models for all of us who live with bipolar disorder.

-The Power of Flexibility and Listening:
As I look back over my life, I discover that it has been a process of growing with positivity. No blinding lights, no booming voice, just a slow, sometimes steady, sometimes not, journey of faith. The only thing that survives has two qualities, deep roots and flexibility, these two assets can serve us well as we continue this process of growing positive with bipolar. The richness of our

tradition, the wisdom of the ages, can serve us as we struggle to discern a calling for each of us to consider.

But we also need to be flexible, to be willing to move in directions we never thought available or appropriate. Part of flexibility is being able to hear and learn to listen, for most of us are so busy talking, too busy doing, we don't hear anything but ourselves. Someone once said, "Prayer doesn't mean to listen to oneself speaking. Prayer involves becoming silent, and being silent, and waiting until God is heard."

If we want to hear from God, it might be better to put ourselves in a position of listening. Sometimes that means being in the right place, sometimes that means being with the right people and sometimes that means just listening a little harder.

-The Power of Sharing:
When we seek for connection, we restore the world to wholeness. Our seemingly separate lives become meaningful as we discover how truly necessary we are to each other. That's the way things come clear. All of a sudden you realize how obvious they've been all along. You are today where your thoughts have brought

you; you will be tomorrow where your thoughts take you. First, it is necessary to stand on your own two feet. But the minute a man finds himself in that position, the next thing he should do is reach out his arms. For the life that no longer trusts another human being and no longer forms ties to the community is not a human life any longer. So, more importantly, we people with bipolar disorder need to build together, a strong positive supportive bond and stand together for common stability.

-The Power of Reflection:
I wonder if without my ritual times, I would appreciate them as much. I wonder if without the sacred rhythms of time and place and action, I would find myself only racing to the next event and forgetting to savor the moment. Ritual action is a way of marking time, of taking notice of transitions. To set aside time each day, each week, to reflect on what has gone on and what is to come, seems to me a vital part of a healthy life. "The unexamined life is not worth living," said Socrates. Do you ever find yourself reflecting on how the year has gone as you put away the Christmas ornaments or clear off the table from Easter dinner? Who has come into your life this year and who has now departed? How have

you served others, served your God, and who has been a blessing to you? These are the questions that rituals help to answer and rhythm defines. Can the bipolar start to find that positive relationship with the rhythms of his/her mood cycles and begin a new life of stability?

A friend of mine once told me, "Whenever you draw a line in the sand and say, 'We're in and you're out' who will be standing on the other side of the line?" There has been a dreadful tendency on the part of a great many of us to want to draw lines. How interesting to think that in drawing these lines, we may have locked ourselves outside. Do we also lock ourselves out with others because we are bipolar?

Longfellow seemed to address the concept of time the best. If we are dealing with bipolar disorder, we can see the positive meaning in the following quote.

"Time is the coin of your life. It is the only coin you have, and only you can determine how it will be spent. Be careful lest you let other people spend it for you. Wisdom doesn't automatically come with old age. Nothing does - except wrinkles. It's true, some wines improve with age, but only if the grapes were good in the first place."

Building techniques come from what you "believe." Man is what he believes. The thing always happens that you really believe in; and the belief in a thing makes it happen. In the province of the mind, what one believes to be true either is true or becomes true. Remember that what you believe will depend very much on what you are. Unless you believe, you will not understand.

Chapter 15:

Famous Musicians, Authors and Celebrities who Influenced My Life

Q...Are there well-known people that you admire in your life that have projected positive thoughts and thereby helped to build a foundation toward your stability with bipolar?

A...I find that so often in the social media age that we live, there are interesting sites/people who will influence our minds (Facebook is good example). Not a day goes by that we see a film trailer, a song that touches the heart and mind, a painting, or a beautiful piece of art work. These songs, movies, art work, etc. give all of us a way to relate and provide us a way to feel good with the famous. There are some feelings I will share from an earlier age in time (before the computer), however, they are not the most important. Some of us enjoy music from the past, while others enjoy the present day music. All of us need this constant positive feedback from the famous. Perhaps, that is where we all become equal in our mental health minds.

Edgar Allen Poe was said to suffer from manic-depressive or bipolar disorder. This would explain the fact that as time went by, his writings became more disturbed, because, for him, the affliction worsened with time. Poe's drinking and smoking problem were more than likely a way of self-medicating. However, because we only have to go on biographies and autobiographies, we cannot be exactly sure if this is the case.

In early January 1984, I was in my very last deep depression, a deep hole I thought I could never climb out of. Then I happened to read Poe's "Pit and The Pendulum".

We all remember the eerie start: "I was sick, sick unto death, with that long agony, and when they at length unbound me, and I was permitted to sit, I felt that my senses were leaving me. The sentence, the dread sentence of death, was the last of distinct accentuation which reached my ears."

After reading the whole story, I told myself, I will climb out of Poe's Pit and never experience his type of depression again. That was the motivating factor for me to start my positive climb out of depression. It took a lot of positive perseverance along with the proper dosage of Lithium to climb that "pit," but I made it out and have never fallen back again.

However, Poe still haunts me at times, but I have avoided his pit for over 28 years. So, it is an honor that I bring to him...a positive thought...that all of us who deal with Edger Allen Poe's bipolar disorder can supersede above his "pit." Just knowing the author's struggles with bipolar, we are still able to consider that his writings were not written in vain.

Perhaps there are songs and musicians that have touched many bipolar hearts as each of us have struggled to overcome the seriousness of depression. Let me express how some of my sad thoughts occurred when four of my favorite musicians sang their songs.

Perhaps, it was the lyrics that produced my melancholy mood.

Neil Diamond singing one of his songs, not well known by many, was very touching for me: Lady Magdalene...I felt that I was always the man "In between" in my life and I always wondered, "What Will Become of the Man In Between?"

"The man in between waits between the two,
Not hearing the lie and not seeing the truth.
Unknowing what is and denying what seems"

Well I know what became of him. That was when I attempted suicide in May of 1984. It seemed that my depression would not let up for me. I struggled for over one year and a half. I lost all hope and reason yet still denying my ability to overcome...The attempt was not in vein, but built positive perseverance and a positive goal toward achieving "episode free emotional stability." I began my journey, and have maintained over 28 years of stability.

Neil Diamond sang a famous song written by Joni Mitchell: Both Sides Now. This song seemed to share his moods with me about changing "clouds." In 1969 I experienced my first year-long depression. My life was changing so fast without understanding what I would next experience...a pending mania? It became evident to me that one could see how "clouds" can be moods, too. Perhaps, I learned a new lesson about clouds (moods). That there are always both sides to them and that I needed to accept their changes and start working toward positive solutions.

"So many things I would have done
Its cloud illusions I recall
I really don't know clouds (moods) at all"

We all can relate to the folk music of Simon & Garfunkel.
I connected their songs with a significant change of course that I chose at that time in my life. At first it was a very enlightened course for the first months of 1970, but then, it became quite delusional and scary; for I was approaching my first manic episode. These songs still carry a deep message and signals of awareness that something was very wrong in my life at that time, if I would have only listened to my support people. Instead, it was inevitable that I came crashing down. I share a few of their words that still flash back in my mind, even today. I have learned to listen to Simon and Garfunkel and enjoy these two old "Masters" positive lessons

learned well.

And truly I had my day with Bridge over Troubled Waters
But I learned "Your time has come to shine, all your dreams are on their way".
And learned "For it will ease my mind"

El Condor Pasa has taught me a positive passivity to continue with my long standing stability.
"Away, I'd rather sail away
Like a swan that's here and gone
A man grows older every day"

It seems to me that almost everyone alive today has heard of Willie Nelson. And we all can relate to his honest homey style old tunes. One old tune goes way back and again I seem to relate to Willie's old tunes that most people have forgotten.
Willie sang *Hands on the Wheel* back in June of 1984 when I was released from the hospital. I promised myself and my wife that we would always live together with a life of stability. I have never looked back, for now my hand's on the wheel...and "I'm going home."
"With a lady they both enjoy.
Now my hand's on the wheel, I've something that's real,
an' I feel like I'm going' home."

"Remember, people will judge you by your actions, not your intentions. You may have a heart of gold, but so does a hard-boiled egg." Anonymous Author.

Over the years, I have had some people say that I have a "Heart of Gold." I have always questioned this phrase. For what did it really mean? Perhaps, people do judge you by your actions. The old saying, "Actions speak louder than words." Or is it that I, "carry my heart on my sleeve." This may point to my HSP (Highly Sensitive Person). However, I have learned to become extroverted in my life as a professional. But I must say that the "root" of my personality is HSP. Now that I have aged and have a tissue aortic replacement valve in my heart, I am just happy to live a contented life The Song, Heart of Gold, sung by Neil Young, gave me a clue as to where and when the Heart of Gold really exists. Perhaps, my positive perseverance has led me to a balanced ageing.
"That keeps me searching for a heart of gold and I'm getting old."

As I have become more aware of the ageing process, from all my research, in general, I have found that bipolar episodes do not increase with age.

Perhaps that is due to moods that seem
to mellow with age. Or, to be at all frank,
at age 70, this bipolar just may have had
enough of those wild mood swings!

Often-times, I have found that I can
enhance my positive thinking from the
wisdom and maturity of many authors. I
have tried to utilize their quotes and
sayings as I continue my journey toward
my positive stability. These are some of
their insights that have taught growth
and character building in my life.

-While learning to deal with bipolar
disorder, one needs to consider how we
deal with the disorder. Might I suggest
"Actions" and not words. Florence
Nightingale says, "ask me why I do not
write something ...I think one's feelings
waste themselves in words; they ought
all to be distilled into actions and to
actions that bring results."

-Thomas A. Richards suggests, if you pay
attention to the darkness, you will never
find the light. If you study and relive
your past experiences, analyzing them,
and getting in touch with your feelings
you will only reinforce those feelings.
One should not focus on negative. Focus
on the good, the positive, the beautiful,
and the nice. A happy person is fully

caught up in the moment -- and is not thinking about the past or the future. Too much thinking and analyzing just makes any problem worse. Today is a wonderful day--live it in the present!

-Perhaps, for a bipolar, taking a "risk" in controlling any onset of a beginning mood swing is the last thing from our mind. However, if we don't even consider "risk", we may never come close to stability. Can we risk it? Thoughts from Diane Frolov, "I guess what I'm trying to say is, I don't think you can measure life in terms of years. I think longevity doesn't necessarily have anything to do with happiness. I mean happiness comes from facing challenges and going out on a limb and taking risks. If you're not willing to take a risk for something you really care about; you might as well be dead."

-Phillip Adams goes on to emphasize that it seems that people have vast potential. Most people can do extraordinary things if they have the confidence or take the risks. Yet most people don't. They sit in front of the "telly" and treat life as if it goes on forever. Our lives improve only when we take chances - and the first and most difficult risk we can take is to be honest with ourselves.

-There are patterns in life that seem to always be 'changing'. Be it with bipolar disorder, or a physiological disorder, it all comes down to acceptance of "reality." Henry Kissinger has advised many that he wrestled with reality for over 40 years, and says, "I'm happy to state I finally won out." He goes on to say the real distinction is between those who adapt their purposes to reality and those who seek to meld reality in the light of their purposes. Reality is that which, when you stop believing in it, doesn't go away.

Perhaps the bipolar needs to seek the proper tools to overcome their symptoms, and by just acquiring the positiveness of "persistence and perseverance," the goal of achieving stability is within reach. Calvin Coolidge provides us with this positive advice. "Nothing in the world can take the place of persistence. Talent will not; nothing is more common than unsuccessful men with talent. Genius will not; unrewarded genius is almost a proverb. Education will not; the world is full of educated derelicts. Persistence and determination alone are omnipotent. The slogan 'Press On' has solved and always will solve the problems of the human race. That which we persist in doing becomes easier, not that the task itself has become easier, but that our ability to perform it has improved. You have to keep plugging away. We are all growing. There is no shortcut. You have to put time into it to build an audience."

Joseph Addison emphases that if you wish success in life, make perseverance your bosom friend, experience your wise counselor, caution your elder brother, and hope your guardian genius. For the bipolar, it is good to remember that by perseverance, the snail reached the ark. We are made to persist. That's how we find out who we are.

The bipolar needs to look at "simplicity." Perhaps, it would be easier to stop striving, to let go of "striving." Try for a change with how we see what's here and now and then to develop contentment without anxiety and fear. These thoughts are encouraged by Henry David Thoreau and Lao-tzu. "Go confidently in the direction of your dreams! Live the life you've imagined. As you simplify your life, the laws of the universe will be simpler. Simplicity is the peak of civilization. Nothing as simple as we hope it will be.
-Manifest plainness,

-Embrace simplicity,
-Reduce selfishness,
-Have few desires.
Try always to adore simple pleasures. They are the last refuge of the complex."

No matter how we perceive ourselves as a bipolar, we must always work toward maintaining our dignity, for it is truly our dignity that builds self-esteem. Remember that being bipolar does not dictate who we are as a person, but by having a solid foundation with dignity, we can achieve at the same level as anyone else.

-John Brown encourages us to be mild with the mild, shrewd with the crafty, confiding to the honest, rough to the ruffian, and a thunderbolt to the liar. But in all this, never be unmindful of your own dignity. And Rabbi Abraham Herschel suggested that self-respect is the fruit of discipline; the sense of dignity grows with the ability to say no to oneself. Dignity comes not from control, but from understanding who you are and taking your rightful place in the world.

-Walter Last has expressed these insights. It is the feelings and emotions, our likes and dislikes that give our life meaning, that make us happy or unhappy, fulfilled or dissatisfied and that to a large degree decide our course of action and even our health. Diseases not only make us feel unwell, but negative and suppressed emotions and feelings are a major contributing factor in causing our diseases. It is only by following your deepest instinct that you can lead a rich life, and if you let your fear of consequence prevent you from following your deepest instinct, then your life will be safe, expedient and thin.

I have learned that feelings and emotions can be the strongest characteristic in the human mind that brings out the total truth and understanding in ones life. If we persist in trying to hide "them", then they will sneak in our back door to show us the way - and the way is to let "them" out. However, there is a need for positive control when a person is dealing with bipolar disorder.

-William Wirt has expressed these thoughts to "seize the moment of excited curiosity on any subject to solve your doubts; for if you let it pass, the desire may never return, and you may remain in ignorance. Only the curious will learn and only the resolute overcome the obstacles to learning. The quest quotient has always excited me more than the intelligence quotient."

-Oscar Wilder suggests that "nowadays most people die of a sort of creeping common sense, and discover when it is too late that the only things one never regrets are one's mistakes.
Perhaps, that is why the person with bipolar needs to always look at all the positive aspects and remember the mistakes they had in the past. What we have to do is to be forever curiously testing new opinions and courting new impressions"

-Frank Tibolt provides us with some choices, expressing that inspiration may be a form of super consciousness, or perhaps of sub consciousness. But I am sure it is the antithesis of self-consciousness. We should be taught not to wait for inspiration to start a thing. Action always generates inspiration. Inspiration seldom generates action. George Bernard Shaw suggests that imagination is the beginning of creation. You imagine what you desire, you will what you imagine, and at last you create what you will. There is only one admirable form of the imagination: the imagination that is so intense that it creates a new reality that it makes things happen.

-Epicurus reminds us that hope doesn't come from calculating whether the good news is winning out over the bad. It's simply a choice to take action. Hope begins in the dark; the stubborn hope that if you just show up and try to do the right thing, the dawn will come. You wait and watch and work: you don't give up. Do not spoil what you have by desiring what you have not; but remember that what you now have was once among the things you only hoped for. The past is a source of knowledge, and the future is a source of hope. Love of the past implies faith in the future. Stephen Ambrose suggests it is difficult to say what is impossible, for the dream of yesterday is the hope of today and the reality of tomorrow.

-Perhaps as we journey through life, we need to find a firm "balance" with bipolar and between the mood changes that occur with the ever changing day. Suggested here by Euripides, the best and safest thing is to keep a balance in your life, acknowledge the great powers around us and in us. If you can do that, and live that way, you are really a wise man. We can be sure that the greatest hope for maintaining equilibrium in the face of any situation rests within ourselves. Johann Wolfgang von Goethe states, "So divinely is the world organized that every one of us, in our place and time, is in balance with everything else. Order is not pressure which is imposed on society from without, but an equilibrium which is set up from within."

-And with a more balanced life, George E. Woodberry suggests that "If you can't have faith in what is held up to you for faith, you must find things to believe in yourself, for a life without faith in something is too narrow a space to live. So faith is closing your eyes and following the breath of your soul down to the bottom of life, where existence and nonexistence have merged into irrelevance. All that matters is the little part you play in the vast drama."

This final quote is one that helped me through one of my deepest depressions. Perhaps it requires totally that positive mind set that this chapter has attempted to reveal from the authors and musicians that were quoted. Now, with Trey Parker and Matt Stone, I ask you to ponder this unique paradox: "I love life...Yeah, I'm sad, but at the same time, I'm really happy that something could make me feel that sad. It's like...It makes me feel alive, you know. It makes me feel human. The only way I could feel this sad now is if I felt something really good before. So I have to take the bad with the good. So I guess what I'm feeling is like a beautiful sadness."

Chapter 16:

Physical Heath Causing Changes in Mental Health

There have been three serious physical issues that have occurred recently in my life.

1). Aortic heart valve replacement surgery, (August 8, 2008).
2). A chest contusion with three broken ribs from falling off my bicycle (May 24, 2010).
3). A diagnostic evaluation of the abdominal and peritoneal cavity (August 31, 2010).

I found that all three of these physical issues required significant challenges with maintaining my positive bipolar attitude and stability.

There have been many family and friends

who have asked me if I am not worried about my heart surgery (aortic valve replacement). I answer by saying that I stay in my "Calm Center," and share some thoughts with them about worry: Worry a little bit every day and in a lifetime you will lose a couple of years. If something is wrong, fix it if you can. But train yourself not to worry. Worry never fixes anything says Mary Hemingway. If you can solve your problem, then what is the need of worrying? If you cannot solve it, then what is the use of worrying? Do not anticipate trouble, or worry about what may never happen. Keep in the sunlight, advises Benjamin Franklin. Worries are thoughts and images of a negative nature in which mental attempts are made to avoid anticipated potential threats. I have learned that what worries you will master you. It has been my positive viewpoint with bipolar to deal with worry by letting go of control. Learn to accept that some things are beyond your ability to control. Once this expectation is gone, you will likely discover a reduction of your stress. I will trust in my days after my heart valve surgery that they will be full of joy, but it is I who will make it that way. Similarly, it is equally important to stay stable and balanced with my bipolar disorder and guard against any adverse triggers. Courage and trust in myself will keep me most positive with this challenge.

I was thinking as I waited for aortic valve replacement surgery, how Stephanie Meyer described how disjointedly time seemed to flow, passing in a blur at times, with single images standing out more clearly than others. And then, at other times, every second was significant, etched in my mind. If we take care of the moments, the years will take care of themselves. Isaac Newton put it this way, it is very strange that the years teach us patience - that the shorter our time, the greater our capacity for waiting. If I have ever made any valuable discoveries, it has owed more to patient attention, than to any other talent. With these thoughts, time and patience was all I needed as I prepared for my (AVR). An aortic angiogram will be performed to monitor the health of my aorta. Then I will meet with my Cardiothoracic Surgeon. But equally important I say that my moods were stable and I feel competent with my bipolar coping skills.

Martha Washington's words have taught me determination. To be cheerful and happy in whatever situation I may be in;

for I have also learned from experience that the greater part of our happiness or misery depends upon our dispositions, and not upon our circumstances. Charles E. Jefferson also reminded me that gratitude is born in hearts that take time to count up past mercies. It was with this "attitude of gratitude" that I continued to count my blessings in my life. My pending aortic valve replacement surgery will give me a healthy heart so to spread positive love to all my friends and family. It will continue to provide that positiveness that will support me and my challenges with bipolar during this time in my life. It took a combination of my own self-confidence and my own knowledge to continue toward my aortic valve replacement surgery. When my wife and I met with my Cardiothoracic Surgeon, it was a positive visit and many questions were answered. He stated that my heart was very healthy except for the "leaking" aortic valve. A tissue valve will replace it and I'm very pleased to say that my moods are staying at a high level of positiveness. Knowledge was also a key to anxiety. I wanted to know more about the surgery, so I met with the allied health professional known as a perfusionist, who works in association with the surgeons to connect the heart/lung pump to my heart. The perfusionist will monitor the machine and is an extremely intelligent and knowledgeable individual.

When the evening before my aortic valve surgery came, I viewed my whole life as but a point in time. My time is here and my time is now. For the point of living and being an optimist, is to be wise enough to believe the best is yet to come. In part, the Optimist Creed has taught me. "To be so strong that nothing can disturb your peace of mind and to be too large for worry, too noble for anger, too strong for fear, and too happy to permit the presence of trouble."

My surgery went well. It was the recovery that put me in hell. Perhaps, it was all the heavy medications used during surgery and ICU, coupled with not receiving my Lithium that caused hallucinations, paranoia, and aggressive mania. For four long days, I was no longer a recovered, stable bipolar with 25 yeas of stability.

The paranoia led me to conclude the doctors and nurses where mounting a very dangerous conspiracy against me. This combined with vivid hallucinations of attacking "black flies" that lasted all of one night. My paranoia then led to an aggressive manic confrontation with the night nurse. I envisioned that she was confiscating the TV remote from me, which held the answers to the conspiracy. So I aggressively held her back and grabbed her procedures papers. She, of course, notified my doctors. The next morning, I had all three doctors (internist, cardiologist, and surgeon) to contend with. Fortunately, they shed some light on the causes of my moods and actions. Once back on my Lithium, after four days of serious bipolar instability, my paranoia and aggressive behavior diminished rapidly.

If it were not for the constant love and compassion of my wife, Linda, it would have taken a lot longer to recover from those mood swings. She was so supporting with the doctors and nurses, at the same time giving me constant knowledge that I would get through all of my mood swings. I knew that I needed to regain my positive attitude as soon as possible. I was pleased with my stability showing no evidence of any bipolar episodes with the final two day stay in the hospital.

What happened? I'm still not quite sure. But I do know that my mood stabilizer medication   (Lithium),   was   not administered for over 48 hours. That, coupled with trying to recover from four body tubes hanging out of my abdomen for four days, were the precipitating factors causing the lapse into bipolar instability and the resultant serious mood swings.

I have learned a lot from this experience of bipolar instability. With my stability continuing to progress and with a positive attitude, I am confident and in complete control.

I am now a firm believer that if your heart is stopped by medical science, that there has to be a large amount of faith in the heart/lung machine to perform its designed duties. We know that the common person has no control when undergoing open heart surgery, therefore, faith in someone or something has to occur. Perhaps, a little more faith in God would provide our trust in the heart/lung machine. Call me simple in my thinking, but the next time you have your heart stopped; you could be questioning the theories of both science vs. religion. By the same reasoning, we as people with bipolar, need to have some faith in how we can retain a positive attitude when having a serious surgical intervention.

After my open heart surgery, exercise and walking was a big necessity. I found that exercise could also increase my positive psychological thoughts. So it came as no surprise that exercise provides psychological and physical benefits. However, if you also adopt a strategy that engages your mind while you exercise, you can get a whole host of psychological benefits fairly quickly.

I was pleased with my mind and body exercises in the next year and a half after surgery, keeping my stability in balance. However, I became aware that a minor change was occurring within my system in May of 2010. Well, with all my past experiences with mood changes, I felt that my "motor" was running a little high. Perhaps there was a synchronicity that was connected to a serious bike fall and my "motor" going a little too fast. Anyway, after the fall, I knew that I fractured some ribs and my wife took me to the ER for x-rays. The doctor's evaluation was that I had chest contusions with three broken ribs, skin and muscles causing significant pain tenderness and swelling, with a lot of purplish discoloration. It was evident that I was going to be very sore for the next couple of weeks. However, I knew my positive attitude needed to give me a firm foundation so that I could slow down for better control of a potential episode. That is something that over time, I have learned when I am flirting with my stability, that there comes an event to put me back into control of my bipolar disorder. You may find the same thing if you remain positive about a serious event.

After two and a half weeks my bruised rib cage had all but healed; though I was told by many that it could take between two to four months to heal. Perhaps my healing processes are different than most others, but I have learned, from past experiences, by keeping a positive attitude with bipolar, that mental stability is achievable. So it is with this positive comparison, that the mind can heal just as the body can heal. Your body responds to the way you think, feel and act. This is often called the "mind/body connection." When you are stressed, anxious or upset, your body tries to tell you that something is not right. It is with this connection/comparison that I attribute my timely healing of my ribs and equally important, a return to my mental stability. It seems that positivity is constantly challenged by negativity. How often do we seem to doubt our own self-confidence and think that events will turn out with a poor outcome?

Three months later my Internist suggested I undergo an abdominal & peritoneal ultrasound to evaluate my descending aorta and my kidneys. I found myself becoming overly apprehensive because I had the aortic valve replacement just two years earlier and because of my longstanding use of Lithium (40 years). I made a comment, which stated an unfair and negative viewpoint of the possible outcome of this ultrasound. Saying "the upshot is that my bipolar disorder may outlive my descending aorta and kidneys." My feeling is that we with bipolar seem to take it for granted that mental health will be the ultimate end.

This was truly a very negative comment on my part. Most people who know me, realize that I always try to project the concept that you can live with bipolar and still be your most positive and optimistic best. My very sweet wife mentioned this comment, knowing I was somewhat despondent, stating: "Keep being positive, it is good for your health! You have just proved that, do you realize that? Don't ever think your stability may outlive you." Stability is not the physical price we pay. It is the catalyst that helps promote our good health. I thank my wife sincerely, for she has come a very long way with overcoming and always dealing positively with my symptoms of bipolar.

Well, my results of the ultrasound checked out just fine. My kidneys are functioning normally. My Internist said she ordered these tests because she likes to stay "insightful" as to how my organs are performing. There was no indication of kidney failure. My Lithium levels are staying within normal levels considering the long standing 40 years of taking a mood stabilizer. The descending aorta is perfect and my artificial aortic "pig" valve is pumping perfectly. My Internist told me that I was probably over prepared for the visit, and that she hoped I continue to be positive about future tests.

It is with these three physical events, this seasoned gentleman has learned to always stay at the most positive and optimistic level with my physical and mental health.

Chapter 17:

Positive Suggestions for Bipolar Management: Psychiatric, Psychological and Psychotherapy Care

"I don't know what to say" is what most people say when they wonder about what to do for a friend in crisis. The truth is there really isn't much to say but there is a whole lot that one can do. What people remember most and are the most helpful are simple actions that indicate our concern. A freshly baked casserole, a shoveled drive, a bouquet of flowers...these are symbols that can speak more fully than our language often allows.

There is something else...to simply be present to someone suffering can be the greatest gift we can give. Be present by simply listening as the sufferer pours out their frustrations, anger, hope or sorrow. Don't seek to provide easy answers or glib conclusions. Be a sponge for their emotions. Spend time just absorbing what they may need to share. All of this takes time, of course. That may be the true mark of friendship...the willingness to sacrifice that most precious commodity.

No one likes to be defined by a chronic condition whether it be asthma, diabetes, arthritis or....bipolar disorder. The fear of immediately and forever being labeled, and the realization that our lifestyle will need to be permanently adjusted, can be terrifying. For some, accepting the diagnosis of bipolar disorder may come as relief. For many though, there is no shortcut to acceptance....it's earned the hard way. What is clear is that everyone's process of coming to terms with and accepting their diagnosis is different. What is evident is that acceptance "leads to stability."

It is no secret that the stigma and discrimination associated with bipolar disorder is a big barrier to one's acceptance. Hollywood's move from their characterizations of unpredictable and more violent people with mental illness was a positive move. They chose to use a more accurate depiction of fully human, multi-dimensional characters, which was well received. The shift, however, to positive portrayals must also be accompanied by accuracy to further the public's perception and education and to undo the damaging stereotypes we're all so familiar with.

We ask ourselves why people relapse...whether there was a non-adherence to medication, or if the early results for Lithium and/or other mood stabilizers were too optimistic. Indeed, Lithium and other mood stabilizers' limitations lead to a re-examination of psychotherapy's role and potential with answers to bipolar disorder. We know that more came out about inheritability of the illness, which led people to look for other treatments.

Over the past decades or so, we have developed several psychotherapies that are specifically designed for the treatment of bipolar disorder. Most of these therapies include: cognitive behavioral therapy (CBT), interpersonal social rhythm therapy (IPSRT), family-focused therapy (FFT) and dialectical behavior therapy (DBT).

We now know that the best treatment for

bipolar disorder includes both a mood stabilizer, which is used to prevent future mood episodes and psychotherapy/counseling, which is used to show people how to manage the symptoms of their disorder/illness. Neither of these works well alone.

Medications are extremely important for stability. I believe it to be the one element that actually directly deals with our bipolar disorder. The right medication can help to balance the chemicals that cause our fluctuations. Unfortunately, we are exposed to many other factors that cause our chemical imbalance to fluctuate, whether they are self-imposed factors like drugs or alcohol, our environment, or changes in our brain or body. Because we are all so different in our chemical makeup, we require individual medication treatment. "Our environment" is about the life we are in the midst of, that we might either be in control of or not. Situations of abuse, poverty, family or personal drug use, absolutely anything that could add stress to our lives. Yes, there will always be something that will cause stress in our lives.

Psychotherapy, talk therapy, behavior modification, responds well to bipolar disorder. However, with circumstances in our environment, for whatever reason, we develop learned behaviors. We do this in response to the way our parents treat us, the way we are taught to deal with things, our exposure to certain people, feelings and situations that have been repressed and manifest into "negative behavior". Eventually we learn to adapt those behaviors to everything in our life. It is our "response" to our life situations. After using those behaviors for so long, we become accustomed to them and believe them to be "just who we are." When our bipolar disorder rears its ugly head, those behaviors take on a new life, but not a pretty life at all. We begin to use our bipolar disorder as an excuse for bad behavior. Once I uncovered and dealt with my manifestations in therapy, my behaviors changed tremendously. I found that my cycles were not nearly as difficult to deal with as they were in years past. The most valuable lesson I discovered and learned was that my learned behaviors were partly a product of my mother and my identical twin brother. So, if I learned from my mother and my brother, my children could certainly learn from me. I was determined to break the cycle of abuse and I did. My children do not behave as I did years earlier and I hope their behaviors are products of my better parenting.

I believe in psychotherapy because I am willing to admit I am a "player" in this game. I have been proactive in my total health care and continue to develop a strong knowledge between the proper mood stabilizing medications and the positive influence of psychotherapy. Behavior modification is learning self-confidence and self-esteem. Recognizing the triggers which may change daily in family life, we can learn to avoid potential negative reaction, stay with a healthy positive attitude, and succeed in warding off an episode. We know that negative reactions will stimulate different biochemical changes within the brain.

In recent years, several types of psychotherapy have emerged that are tailored specifically to treat Bipolar Disorder, or have been adapted for this purpose:

Cognitive Behavioral Therapy (CBT) is based on the theory that how we perceive situations influences how we feel emotionally. Depressed patients seemed to experience spontaneous negative thoughts that focused on oneself, the world, or the future. It was then the goal to teach patients skills to identify distorted thinking, modify those beliefs and relate to others in healthier ways.

CBT targeted for bipolar, patients learn skills to enable them to take their medication regularly, sleep and rise at regular times, and set manageable goals. (Learning Positive Rituals and Rhythms).They also learn to manage any residual symptoms of depression or mania that may occur between episodes.

In Family Focused Therapy (FFT), the therapist educates the patient about the condition, including how stress can affect the illness and the importance of maintaining a consistent daily routine. The therapist also helps the patient maintain healthy relationships with loved ones.

Interpersonal Social Rhythm Therapy (IPSRT) is used to address episodes linked to noncompliance with medication, stressful life events, or disruptions in wake/sleep cycles and one's daily routine. In IPSRT, the therapist helps the patient to discover a regular daily routine, thus stabilizing the mood. Once a set routine has been established, therapy turns to interpersonal relationships....in particular, identifying when event(s) sparked the most recent mood episode and then working to resolve the issue.

One type of psycho-education is known as a medication group, which combines group therapy and teaching the participants about the medications they are taking. The goal is to increase medication compliance and decrease incidence of re-hospitalization.

Dialectical Behavior Therapy (DBT) can be used to treat bipolar disorder. It is a form of cognitive behavioral therapy and teaches mindfulness techniques to stay in the present moment, interpersonal skills to communicate more effectively and assertively, and methods to cope with tolerating distressing situations that have no immediate resolution.

A newer program called MIDAA (Mental Illness Drug Addiction and Alcoholism). This program will develop and integrate treatments across systems. It is a program designed to bring treatments together from both sides of the spectrum and implement it in one program for people with dual diagnosis.

Perhaps there is a possible need to

integrate our vast knowledge of medical psychiatry and the "retooling" of psychotherapy as we see it today:

For the most part, these new psychotherapies (CBT, FFT, IPSRT, DBT) take a nuts-and-bolts approach...such as teaching patients how to keep a daily routine and rhythm. It's essential to take medication regularly, how to manage symptoms of the illness that persist between episodes, how to recognize early symptoms and seek help; all before the illness spins out of control.

-In therapy the patient also works at repairing broken relationships, resolving financial woes, and dealing with job loss, any and all of which can follow a prolonged episode.

-Medication can help control symptoms, but it does not help fix relationships or get a job back. That is where therapy comes in. Therapists can help reinforce the psychiatrist's instructions and troubleshoot any problems with medication adherence. It is important to choose the right therapist, how long therapy will last and what type of chemistry you need to develop between yourself and your therapist. Perhaps, by keeping this dialog somewhat generic, we will learn more and it will be informative.

-Therapy is an investment of time, money and emotional energy. It is suggested to meet with a potential therapist to find out "how they do therapy". At the end of an hour, you decide if you want to come back or not. It is important that you feel that the therapist is "open". Don't get discouraged if the same therapist a friend raved about leaves you cold. It's really about fit. Psychotherapy is a collaborative effort between therapist and patient. Ask each potential therapist what he or she thinks you need help with, the type of therapy they practice, and whether it has been proven to be effective in people with bipolar disorder. Goals are important. You need a clear idea of what you are working on. For a lot of people it is depression. For others it's social rhythm. For some, it is learning how to recognize early warning signs of mania.

-There is no magic formula for determining how long therapy will take. Most people don't need to continue indefinitely. Knowing that you have been stable for a while is a good reason to discontinue therapy. People who are doing well (generally) continue to do well. When a patient is ready to stop altogether, most therapists will encourage him or her to return if they need a "tune up." It is good for a patient to call once or twice a year if they have a particular stressor. Just as the need for therapy may wax or wane over one's lifetime, the type of therapy that's needed may change, too.

-What about chemistry? Do you feel your therapist is condescending? Are you reluctant to try their therapies? These may be signs that your relationship is not working. Be careful against dropping a therapist too hastily. If you are not comfortable with the therapist, rather than give up; try to make the alliance stronger. This shows your own self-confidence.

-Unfortunately, those most in need of therapy are the most likely to drop out. However, the problem may be the fault of the therapist. People just don't come back. The therapist needs a call system. It could be that the patient is very depressed, and just can't get out of bed. Most therapists have found that people greatly appreciate the call.

Recent studies suggest that talk therapy

may be as good as or better than drugs in the treatment of depression, but fewer than half of depressed patients now get such therapy compared with the vast majority 20 years ago. Insurance company reimbursement rates and policies that discourage talk therapy are part of the reason.

Several factors play a part in the treatment of a person with bipolar. There are three professionals specializing in talk therapy: psychiatrists, psychologists, and clinical social workers.

I have discussed the theory, treatment and control of bipolar disorder. In general most health care professionals seem to have a good handle on the modalities of bipolar disorder. In fact, most have done extensive research on the different medications for recurrent and cyclic mood changes. However, there are many psychological, self-help and behavioral treatments that provide excellent help and support the positive aspects of dealing with bipolar disorder.

Some questions still seem to linger with most people with bipolar. How long someone must take a psychotherapeutic medication depends on the disorder. Many depressed and anxious people may need medication for a single period, perhaps for several months, and then never have to take it again. But, for the bipolar, medication may have to be taken indefinitely or, perhaps, intermittently. Like any medication, psychotherapeutic medications do not produce the same effect in everyone. Some people may respond better to one medication than another. Some may need larger dosages than others do. Some experience annoying side effects, while others do not. Age, sex, body size, body chemistry, physical illnesses and their treatments, diet, and habits such as smoking, are some of the factors that can influence a medications effect.

Herein lies some of the questions that people with bipolar, who are still dealing with a lack of stability, may be concerned about. Why do I still seem to be experiencing depression too many times throughout the year? Why can't I tell that I am going into a hypomania again? Why am I feeling fatigued and have no energy? Why do I have so much trouble with sleeping? Why do I need to take 2 or 3 different types of medications in order to sleep?

It is interesting that most of these people have stated they have been in control and have achieved a level of stability with their bipolar disorder. Yet, when there is a review of some of their comments shared by them on a personal level, they reveal just the opposite. Perhaps this is the makeup of the bipolar. Is it a subconscious need to hang on to a disorder that does not yet have a cure? Or is it a denial that somehow they cannot seem to ultimately help themselves, or even learn to "think" positively about dealing with bipolar disorder?

The most positive important goal for a person with bipolar expression is "balance," proper channeling of psychic and physical energy. Many times the physical element is addressed only through medication which works in the brain cells. But remember the importance of the endocrine system. Proper functioning of the endocrine cells is as important as brain cell function. Body systems are interdependent and must be treated that way.

Physical exercise which maintains cardiovascular function can keep the endocrine system in "balance" and is imperative for people with bipolar expression. In addition, psychotherapeutic process must be sought to remove energy blocks from the consciousness. Everyone, regardless of his personal experience of childhood, sustains psychic trauma. Everyone has some blockage in the chakras. The seven chakras are the energy centers in our body and brain in which energy flows through.

When psychological blocks are removed and physical knots in the body are worked out through exercise, energy can flow and heal the parts of the individual which are in need. The spiritual practice of Reiki releases emotional, physical, psychological, and spiritual pain. It helps in the facilitation of healing. Then growth can occur.

Andy Osborne has written about how yin yang illustrates the key elements of bipolar disorder by the classic black-and-white yin yang symbol. The unique way that it correlates with bipolar disorder allows a symbolic yet highly practical and revealing analysis of the disorder's main symptoms.

Long before a diagnosis of bipolar disorder was possible, ancient Chinese thinkers recognized a stark duality pervading natural phenomena such as day and night, as well as such ideas as harmony and balance between opposing elements of human nature, which they used the yin-yang symbol to represent.

People with bipolar disorder experience distinct mood episodes, or "mood swings. The yin and yang represent the two extremes in mood that exist within one person...similar to how both black and white exist within the confines of the yin yang's circular boundary.

The mood cycles of bipolar disorder often last for months at a time, often causing the person suffering from the disorder to seem to others to be possessed by two personalities. However, bipolar disorder is not a problem of shifting personalities, but of opposing moods. A bipolar can remain aware of his identity and illness even as his moods cycle between mania and depression.

Classic Chinese philosophers recognized the two phases of bipolar disorder individually, using the word "kuang" to refer to mania and "dian" to depression. However, the two conditions were not recognized as two sides of a single mental disorder. Dr. Jiang speculates that this is due to the fact that mania was more destructive in the way it manifested itself in people than depression.

Correlations between the yin and yang and depression were indeed made by ancient Chinese philosophers. According to Acupuncture Today, the Qing dynasty thinker Ye Tian Shi equated depression with a deficiency of the "qi" (energy) of a person's yang, causing the darker side to dominate the white yin, leading to decreased energy and other symptoms of depression. Perhaps the ancient Chinese were really looking for the quality of positiveness to support the negative darker side involved with decreased energy of the symptoms of depression.

Perhaps the ancient Chinese were looking for a support between mania and depression, a "balance" between positivity and negativity so that the two different moods could somehow be a positive "oneness."

There is a tried and true slogan to help us to stay in touch with our feelings and needs. Sometimes the onset of anxiety or a sudden drop in mood can be traced to our having forgotten to eat so our blood sugar levels are off kilter. Sometimes we may be carrying resentment or feeling lonely, or we are just too tired. Taking a little time out from our busy day to ask ourselves if we are feeling too hungry, angry, lonely, or tired, gets us in touch with our feelings. When we know what we are feeling we can make choices and take the appropriate action to get our needs for food, companionship or rest.

Being too hungry, angry, lonely, or tired, are conditions that leave us more vulnerable to the temptations that lead us away from our program of dual recovery. Part of recovery is learning to pay attention to these inner signals and practice appropriate ways to meet our needs and resolve issues in a manner that will enhance our abstinence and serenity.

Now, I would like to summarize a few thoughts by Afik Yusof, as he appropriately suggested some words for the management and enlightenment of bipolar disorder:

"Whatever feeling you have within you, is attracting tomorrow. Worry attracts more worry. Anxiety attracts more anxiety. Unhappiness attracts more unhappiness. Dissatisfaction attracts more dissatisfaction.
AND
Joy attracts more joy. Happiness attracts

more happiness. Peace attracts more peace. Gratitude attracts more gratitude. Kindness attracts more kindness. Love attracts more love. Your job is an inside one. To change your world, all you have to do is change the way you feel inside. How easy is that?"

Chapter 18:

The Present Positive Management for Bipolar Disorder

Q...What have you found to be the most positive current treatment and management of bipolar disorder, and research that may lead to a possible cure?

A...Mostly, the present management and treatment technique of bipolar disorder is a positive approach to taking medication. The key is reducing the frequency and severity of mood episodes. However, bipolar medications are most effective when used in conjunction with therapy and healthy lifestyle choices, including diet, exercise and support networks. These factors play an important role in managing symptoms of mania and depression and will also determine how much medication is required.

Both the psychiatrist and the patient need to be positive about working together in order to find the right bipolar medication and dose. Most people respond to medication differently, thus several drugs might be tried before one is successful in a particular case. It may also take some time to establish the optimal dose. This is crucial since the medication should be re-evaluated on a regular basis because the optimal dose fluctuates along with changes in a lifestyle. Medication should be continued even if a person feels better as the likelihood of having a relapse is very high.

All prescription drugs come with risks, but if taken responsibly and, especially if combined with therapy and healthy lifestyle, the risks will be minimized and the efficiency of the treatment maximized. There are three positive solutions to taking medications responsibly:

- Medication is taken as prescribed.
-Track of side effects is noted and recorded.
-Being aware of potential drug interactions.

Common mood stabilizers used in the treatment of bipolar disorder are:

1) Lithium, which is the oldest (approved by the FDA in 1971) and most well-known mood stabilizer, highly effective for treating mania. It can also help bipolar depression however it is not as effective for mixed episodes or rapid cycling. Lithium takes from one to two weeks to reach its full effect. When Lithium is taken, it is important to have serum Lithium blood tests to make sure the dose is in the therapeutic range. (0.6 mmol/L – 1.04 mmol/L).

2) Anticonvulsants, which have been shown to relieve the symptoms of mania and reduce mood swings. These include:
-Valproic acid (Depakote) – often the first choice for rapid cycling, mixed mania or mania with hallucinations or delusions.

-Carbamazepine (Tegretol)
-Lamotrigine (Lamictal)
-Topiramate (Topamax)

3) Natural Mood Stabilizers

-Herbalmax Mood & Fatigue Formula
-Omega 3 fatty acid
-St. John's Wart

-MoodCalm Native Remedies

4) Other medications used in treatment of bipolar include:

-Antidepressants, however their use is becoming increasingly controversial. The bottom line overall here: antidepressants may carry much more risk for people with bipolar disorder than is generally recognized. That antidepressants can cause "switching", bringing on a manic or hypomanic phase, is generally accepted.

-Antipsychotics-Benzodiazepines – fast acting sedatives that work within 30 minutes to an hour. These might be prescribed while a person is waiting for the medication to start reacting; however, these are also highly addictive so they should be used only as a 'temporary measure'.

Research has found that people who take medication for bipolar disorder tend to recover much faster and control their moods much better if they also receive psychotherapy. Therapy helps with coping strategies, monitoring the progress, and dealing with problems that the disorder is causing in the life of a bipolar.

Since Lithium has been considered the 'old stand by' for bipolar I, the present information by Candida Fink, MD adds some very positive light on the most up to date information about this mood stabilizer. Some patients often have a misconception of the long standing usage of Lithium, however it is still an excellent starting mood stabilizer because it is one of the best tested, longest used (since 1971) and most effective intervention for bipolar I. It is the only mood stabilizer that's proven to reduce the risk of suicide in bipolar disorder.

There was a long period of time in recent history when doctors were leaning toward using the newer medications to treat mania and bipolar disorder, but as experiences with those medicines have revealed a number of difficult side effects, psychiatrists are moving back to the old standby, Lithium. While Lithium has its own side effects, they are well defined and can often be reduced or eliminated with adjustments and modifications to dose or other straightforward interventions. Following are the most common side effects: Stomach problems, weight gain, frequent urination, kidney damage, liver damage, foggy thinking, fatigue and tremor.

Lithium is a naturally occurring salt that just happens to calm the nerves and, when used under a doctor's supervision, has manageable side effects for most people. One of the biggest challenges with Lithium is that blood levels (the concentration of Lithium in the blood) must be maintained in a very narrow range. If the Lithium level dips below its therapeutic level, the drug isn't effective. If it rises too high, the drug can become toxic, and severe Lithium toxicity can lead to death. Therefore, it is mandatory to:

-Always take the prescribed dose. Appropriate doses can vary widely from person to person – even people of similar weights. The blood level is the important number in the case of Lithium.

-A prescribed regular blood test is needed to check your Lithium levels – at least every few months (more regularly when you first start taking it). The "right level" (therapeutic level) is typically between 0.6 and 1.2 mmol/L but every lab has a slightly different range. And while most people require a level in this range, some people do well in a lower range.

-Your doctor may also order additional

blood and urine tests, particularly to check on your thyroid and kidney function.

-Lithium levels can rise as you lose fluid, so be wary of hot weather and vigorous exercise, and limit your consumption of diuretics, including coffee and alcohol.

-If you experience diarrhea, vomiting, dizziness, lack of coordination, blurred vision, or other signs of Lithium toxicity, contact your doctor immediately. If you can't reach your doctor, head to the nearest emergency room.

-A form of Lithium purported to be safer: Lithium orotate. The theory behind this claim is that the chemical compound delivers Lithium to the brain more efficiently than Lithium carbonate, the standard compound, so it requires less Lithium in your bloodstream to be effective. However, no studies currently show that Lithium orotate is effective in treating mania or depression.

Twenty-five to 35 years ago, most people diagnosed with bipolar disorder were middle-age adults who had distinct euphoric episodes. Today, most people identified with bipolar disorder present a remarkably different picture of the condition: not only is depression the most pervasive feature of the illness, the manic phase can be a mix of irritability, anger and depression, with or without euphoria.

Today the average age of onset of bipolar disorder is 19. It's not clear whether there is a rising incidence of the disorder in younger people or it is just being recognized more in children and adolescents.

Should a manic be lucky enough to learn that his/her suffering has a name and an array of treatment possibilities, there are still formidable hurdles. Still, there are sufferers who are noncompliant with the prescribed medications. The problem may not always lie with the patient, although the manic-side energy and impaired judgment provide powerful incentives to skip medication. Getting the disorder under control typically requires use of multiple drugs, each with an array of side effects from weight gain to cognitive dulling. Prescribing tolerable drugs in tolerable dosages for each case is a psychiatric high-wire act.

In the summer of 2003, FDA approved the anti-seizure drug lamotrigine (Lamictal) for bipolar disorder. It is the first drug since Lithium to be approved for long-term maintenance treatment of bipolar disorder. Studies indicate that the anticonvulsant delays significantly the occurrence of repeat episodes, — especially depression. What has many psychiatrists especially excited is that the drug appears to be a new kind of mood stabilizer, that is, a mood-elevating mood stabilizer. This is a positive improvement because previous mood stabilities were able to only bring people down from mania. With Lamictal, it is now possible to stabilize mood from below, bringing the person up from depression. Unlike most other drugs for bipolar disorder, Lamictal seems to cause few side effects and is well tolerated by patients. There's no weight gain, no drowsiness, no cognitive dulling, no hormonal changes. And no blood tests are required for continued treatment. The only potentially serious problem is a kind of skin rash, but evidence indicates it is averted if doctors start the drug at extremely low doses. Lamictal, however, has more success with bipolar II patients and not as successful with bipolar I patients.

Exactly how Lamictal works is not clear. The drug was approved for epilepsy nearly a decade ago. On the grounds that there seem to be similar electrical processes at work in the brain in both disorders, anything that works against epilepsy is now tried in bipolar disorder. It is a fact that every effective mood stabilizer blocks the brain process known as kindling, a sensitizing of nerve cells so that they react to even minor provocations with a full-blown mood episode. All mood stabilizers curb hyperactive signaling in pathways that lead from neurotransmitter receptors to the nerve cell interior.

There is a very informative and highly positive account of the neuro-psychiatric drugs used in bipolar disorder. This would be very helpful to any individuals who were not well informed by their psychiatrist about the history and mechanism of action of these mood stabilizers. Although medication regimens vary from individual to individual, Lamictal being a break through mood stabilizer, it may disappointingly, do nothing for some individuals' depression. Yet some are taking both Lithium and Lamictal in quite high dosages and the combination of the two being prescribed is common. However, Lamictal does not cause cognitive dulling, a definite 'perk'.For the most part, psychotherapy combined with psychiatry is a definite must.

It seems there has always been confusion about "mood stabilizers" and bipolar disorder. So I would like to take this positive approach to summarize what they are, their actions, and side effects.

They include Lithium, Depakote (divalproex), Tegretol (carbamazepine) and Lamictal (lamotrigine). In a strict definition, the only true mood stabilizer is Lithium. The other three are anticonvulsant drugs that just happen to work well for bipolar disorder management, but they are all called mood stabilizers in terms of bipolar disorder use. Lithium, Depakote and Tegretol are anti manic drugs, while Lamictal is used for bipolar depression (bipolar II). Someone with bipolar disorder may take multiple drugs at once, such as a combination of Lithium for bipolar mania and Lamictal for bipolar depression.

Mood stabilizers are notorious for a variety of side effects. They are the most effective anti manic drugs on the market, which is why most people with bipolar 1 need to remain on mood stabilizers, indefinitely. Lithium is often prescribed first as it is inexpensive and an excellent drug when it works. Common Lithium side effects include tremors (sometimes excessive), excessive thirst, memory loss and difficulty reading. Toxicity can also lead to kidney problems, and so monitoring Lithium blood levels is needed. The most common side effects of Depakote and Tegretol are weight gain, headache, nausea, dizziness, drowsiness, eye problems and unsteadiness. Weight gain is more often the one people can't tolerate, but when the alternative is mania and possible hospitalization, some people prefer to deal with it.

Possible Lamictal side effects include shortness of breath, neck problems, jerky body movements, itching and a skin rash. There are two kinds of potential rashes associated with Lamictal. One is benign and simply itches. The other is very serious and produces itchy sores. Treatment must be stopped if the second one occurs. Micro dosing may help prevent both types of Lamictal rash. Lamcital does not cause weight gain and the side effects tend to get better over time.

Staying in the positive approach, it is a necessity to discuss the managing of bipolar medications side effects in more detail. Candida Fink, MD had a very good and positive article. This is in part what she said:

One of the main reasons that people with bipolar disorder stop taking their medications is because they simply can no longer tolerate the negative side effects. Nobody likes to gain 30 pounds, feel groggy all day, become forgetful, walk around feeling dizzy, shake, twitch, feel nauseous, or have an anxiety attack. Yet, all of these side effects and more are possible with one medication or another used to treat bipolar symptoms.

From a positive point of view, there are a number of techniques for controlling some of the worst side effects. Not all of them are perfect, but the strategies described here, can frequently reduce or even eliminate negative side effects.

Do not try any of the techniques offered here without first consulting with your physician/psychiatrist. They are offered only as possible ideas for discussion.

When one experiences a particularly unpleasant side effect, a common impulse is to stop or change the medications on your own. Try to avoid this at all costs—talking to you doctor is the best way to manage the side effects without causing further problems. Something else completely unrelated to the medication may be going on, and your doctor can help you sort it all out. If a medication adjustment is required, he or she can also assist you with making those changes. Before you begin taking a new medication, ask your doctor to explain the most common and serious side effects, so you know what to watch out for and what to do if you notice a particular side effect.

When you first start taking a medication, side effects tend to be more common, because your body must get acclimated to the new substance you are ingesting. By comparison: when your exercise routine is too fast, it can make you feel ill, just as starting out with full doses of a medication can cause imbalances in your system.

Your doctor will probably increase the dosage gradually to help you avoid or diminish the intensity of the side effects. Don't increase the medication any faster than is recommended. And if you don't feel well as you are increasing the dose, ask your doctor if you can increase even more slowly.

If you typically take a medication in the morning, and it makes you too drowsy for work, your doctor may recommend that you take it in the afternoon or evening. If you cannot sleep when you take a particular medication at night, your doctor may recommend taking it earlier in the day.

One of the most common strategies used to reduce side effects is to reduce dosage. After adjusting medication doses upward to get the desired effect, you can sometimes back down a bit without losing the benefit. This isn't always possible, but it is often one of the first things your doctor will suggest.

Many medications come in extended-release tablets that release the medication to your bloodstream gradually rather than all at once. Consult your doctor concerning your options.

If no extended-release version of the medication exists, your doctor may recommend that instead of taking one large dose, you take two or more smaller doses throughout the day. This makes taking the medication less convenient, but it may help alleviate the side effects.

If you experience weight gain on Depakote, your doctor may prescribe Topamax in an attempt to reduce weight gain. A positive approach to weight gain is to recommend dieting and exercising more, which is certainly an option. Such suggestions usually come from people who haven't experienced a persistent weight problem, or don't know just how frustrating it is to gain 30 or 40 pounds due to a medication that's supposed to make you feel better.

If you are uncomfortable adding more medications and want to pursue more dietary and exercise strategies, then your doctor may have you consult with a nutritionist or physical therapist, who can give you some ideas on small changes that you might be able to make to at least reduce some of these effects.

If a medication causes intolerable side effects, your doctor may wean you off your current medication and prescribe a new medication that's less likely to produce the same side effect.

Some medications can dry out your mouth, and if you have to talk during the day, this can become very annoying. Sucking on a sugar-free lozenge or sipping water throughout the day can help, but if it becomes too much of a problem, you may want to consult your doctor about other options.

Your local pharmacy probably has some over-the-counter products specifically developed for reducing dry mouth— dental rinses and such. Ask your pharmacist about what is available.

If you are on Lithium, be very cautious about changing your water intake drastically in any direction—up or down. Even taking small sips, if you are doing it all day, could be enough to change the Lithium concentration in your blood and change the effects. Reducing your fluid intake can increase the blood level and create Lithium toxicity.

Although medication is the first-line treatment for bipolar depression and mania, it is not the only treatment. By combining medication with various types of therapies, including psycho-education (books, tapes, and so on), cognitive behavioral therapy, interpersonal and social rhythm therapy, and relationship and family therapy, you may be able to reduce your reliance on medications alone, which could result in fewer side effects.

There are some situations, however, that are potential emergencies. If you experience any of the following side effects, call your doctor immediately:

Overheating or dehydration: If you feel hot, dizzy, or faint, head to a cooler area or take a cool shower or bath and drink plenty of fluids.

Chest pain, shortness of breath, or persistent elevated or irregular heart beats: These symptoms could be related to a number or possible side effects or blood level problems and are medical emergencies.

Skin reactions: Allergies and skin reactions can happen with any medication and should be reported immediately. Some medications can cause severe and dangerous skin conditions.

Seizures or loss of consciousness: seizures and loss of consciousness may be related to various medication side effects and should be considered a medical emergency.

Involuntary muscle movements: Some medications can cause muscle reactions that need to be addressed before they become long-term problems.

Suicidal thoughts, severe agitation or worsening of your symptoms: although these are not necessarily side effects of any medication, some medications may aggravate your bipolar symptoms or simply fail to treat them, leading to thoughts of suicide or other negative emotional and behavioral symptoms.

Remember, you don't have to simply tough it out when you experience side effects. Always taking the positive approach will give you the advantage.

Now, it is important to discuss positive approaches to understanding the therapeutic range for serum Lithium and its significance for management of bipolar disorder. Normal therapeutic range: 0.7 to 1.2, although some labs report ranges at .06 to1.4.

Several large research studies have been done looking at relapse rates (episodes) and relating those rates to people's blood levels at the time. In the biggest such study, the one that really defined the bottom of this range, patients with levels of 0.7 and up had significantly lower relapse rates than those with 0.5 and less. So generally, in bipolar I, it is preferable to acquire a blood level of 0.7 or higher (limiting at 1.0 or 1.2) to be sure the person is protected. If a person has continuous symptoms, one can basically forget about the lower number, because you are going to go by their symptoms, not some reference range. In deciding what is enough dosage, however, she or he still needs lab testing to make sure that his/her blood level doesn't go too high. This is generally the case in bipolar II.

Now, as in my personal case, if my serum Lithium (personal) therapeutic history is extremely well documented,(and it is), then my level at .08 is my base line. Any level dropping below .08 will indicate the possibility that an episode may occur (and a change in side effects). For example, when the therapeutic level dropped to .02, mania could be induced. However, when my blood level increased above .08 to 1.2, my hand tremors increased, and increased creatinine levels in the kidney appeared. This type of Lithium monitoring requires a positive and open communication with my internist and me, in order to produce accurate controls over the serum Lithium and consistent potential episodes along with controlling increases of side effects and organ changes in my body.

Continuing to be positive about how a bipolar who is taking Lithium long term, it is important to monitor kidney functions and thyroid functions. Lithium can be toxic to the kidneys when the serum Lithium blood levels rise over 1.4 and higher when it is taken long term. One of the first signs of these kidney problems can be an increased need to urinate. Taking a positive proactive approach, the creatinine level, in the kidney, may be found to be high. It is then necessary to consider a change in the Lithium dosage. However, a frank discussion is necessary between the doctor and patient on the best possible positive methods of controlling Lithium and kidney functions. There needs to be a positive compromise to find that lowered Lithium dosage, yet still stay in a workable therapeutic range for patient stability. Also find a safe reduction in kidney problems due to the Lithium.

It is necessary to find a positive proactive solution to another side effect with Lithium. One of the most annoying side effects of Lithium can be tremors. Adverse reactions of tremors may be encountered as serum blood levels rise from 1.0 to1.5. These hand tremors may also occur during initial therapy for the acute manic phase, and may persist throughout treatment. The hand tremor associated with Lithium therapy is usually a fine rapid intentional tremor. As the dose and blood level go up, the tremors are common. However, they can often be controlled with low doses of "Propranolol", a blood pressure medication, if you and your doctor decide to continue Lithium at a therapeutic dose. When Propranolol is used to treat tremors, angina (chest pain) and hypertension (high blood pressure) are more unwanted side effects from the Propranolol that can make it a poor choice.

After I had my heart surgery (aortic valve replacement), my cardiologist discussed hawthorn herb extract with me. Hawthorn is known as the heart herb for its many benefits as a heart tonic. Hawthorn herb is especially good where the whole herb needs to be taken. A primary remedy in the treatment of tremors when there are chronic tremors in the hands and the feeling of constant shaking. More research disclosed that hawthorn is a strong circulatory stimulant antioxidant effective in the treatment of Parkinson's and hand tremors.

Looking again for positive solutions, in my personal case, I found a high correlation between my Lithium serum blood level and the onset of my hand tremors. My base line Lithium blood level is 0.8. However, if it would go up to 1.0 or 1.2, my tremors would occur. There are a number of reasons why my blood level would raise, uncontrolled triggers causing my tremors to increase. By using hawthorn, there seemed to be a reduction in tremors. However, although reduced, they were still evident, and not until my blood levels would go down to my 0.8 base line, would the tremors disappear. The use of hawthorn extract is, of course, not FDA approved, but is well documented in the research for heart therapy. More research is needed for why it seems to help some people using Lithium and the onset of tremors when the blood levels rise above 1.2.

Another need for taking a positive view of depression is how to make sense of it from a neuro-biological perspective. Most people with bipolar think of depression in terms of a contemporary pharmacology-based "medical model," the core of which is the idea that depression is an "illness" resulting from "chemical imbalances". From this perspective, the actual feelings and experiences that depressed individuals have are of relatively little interest, either therapeutically or in terms of trying to better understand depression. The principle task is to find ways to "correct" the underlying disturbed pharmacological pattern.

Perhaps there are certain pharmacological correlates to depression, and a fuller understanding of both depression and ways to treat it. This depends fundamentally on paying more attention to individual feelings and experiences. Also to observations made and reported "from the inside." Treating depression pharmacologically will be gained since new pharmacological treatments became available. So some pharmacological treatments can be helpful for some people at some times but no pharmacological agent are effective for all people at all times. Perhaps, it is inconceivable that there is any fixed relation between pharmacological profile and behavioral state in individuals, much less that the same relation holds across different human populations. Equally important, one's mental state is a function not only of pharmacological and external variables, but also of things going on inside one's internal feelings and experiences. Pharmacological agents can of course influence these interactions.

So, where does one go from here? There is clearly, in both respects, a need to move beyond the purely pharmacological approach to something both subtler and more individualized. "Talk therapy" existed prior to the development of contemporary pharmacological approaches. We may be losing them as a body of expertise and a source of continuing insights precisely when the need for them, is becoming most evident. Pharmacological approaches combined with talk therapy requires a clear need to understand how the two relate to one another, how they can best be used in a complementary way, and what their joint efficacy is telling us about what depression actually is. It is becoming clearer that talk therapies, like pharmacotherapy, produce observable effects on the brain and that in some respects the effects on the brain are similar. Even more interestingly, there are suggestions that while talk therapy (cognitive behavioral therapy in this case) and pharmacotherapy produce similar changes in some areas of the brain, they do so by influencing, in different ways, other areas of the brain.

Perhaps we need approaches to treating depression in ways that are subtler and more individualized. Indeed, such an approach would acknowledge that depression is not necessarily, in all cases, best regarded as an "illness" or defect in the individual that needs to be "repaired."

Are drugs useful for depression? Perhaps, on a part time basis. Is talk therapy useful? Yes of course, sometimes. Is there more to depression than a chemical imbalance? Are one's own feelings and experiences significant in depression? Yes, always. Are there other means to learn about depression, when dealing with depression? A positive view point is unquestionably, yes!

Would intensive psychotherapy be more effective than brief therapy for treating bipolar disorder? A study of patients taking medications to treat bipolar disorder, indicated they are likely to get well faster and stay well if they receive intensive psychotherapy, according to results from the Systematic Treatment Enhancement Program for Bipolar Disorder (STEP-BD), funded by the National Institutes of Health's (NIH) National Institute of Mental Health (NIMH).

"STEP-BD is helping us identify the best tools—both medications and psychosocial treatments—that patients and their clinicians can use to battle the symptoms of this illness," said NIMH Director Thomas R. Insel, M.D.

Psychotherapy, together with medication is often used to treat bipolar illness. In addition to examining the role of medication, STEP-BD compared several types of psychotherapy to pinpoint the most effective treatments and treatment combinations.

In a study of 293 participants already taking medication for their bipolar disorder, researchers at the University of Colorado tested the effectiveness of three types of intensive, nine-month-long psychotherapies compared to a control group that received a three-session, psycho educational program called collaborative care. The intensive therapies were:

-Family-focused therapy, which involved patients' family members and focused on enhancing family coping, communication and problem-solving.

-Cognitive behavioral therapy, which

focused on helping the patient understand distortions in thinking and activity, and learn new ways of coping with the illness.

-Interpersonal and social rhythm therapy which focused on helping the patient stabilize his or her daily routines with sleeping cycles, and solve key relationship problems.

-The researchers compared patients' time to recover, and their stability over one year.
Over the course of the year, 64 percent of those in the intensive psychotherapy groups had become well, compared with 52 percent of those in collaborative care therapy. Patients in intensive psychotherapy also became well an average of 110 days faster than those in collaborative care. In addition, patients who received intensive psychotherapy were one and a half times more likely to be clinically well during any month out of the study year than those who received collaborative care. About a third of those in each group dropped out of the study. None of the three intensive psychotherapies appeared to be significantly more effective than the others, although rates of recovery were higher among those in family-focused

therapy compared to the other groups.

"Intensive psychotherapy, when used as an adjunctive treatment to medication, can significantly enhance a person's chances for recovering from depression and staying healthy over the long term," said David Miklowitz, Ph.D., of the University of Colorado. "It should be considered a vital part of the effort to treat bipolar illness."

NAMI has been the leader in helping people with bipolar and other mental illness who can't afford private therapy. They suggest group, online support, and community programs.

William Knoedler, M.D., directed and worked as the psychiatrist for the Program of Assertive Community Treatment (PACT) in Madison, Wisconsin, from 1972-1997. PACT has directors similar to this program in many states:

The founders of PACT tailored the way services are delivered to meet the needs of people with severe mental illnesses. With an assertive, persistent, practical approach, they saw to it that consumers actually received services in a continuous fashion over a number of years. The team doesn't wait until a person comes to the office. The majority of services are delivered where consumers live, work, and spend their leisure time, not in the program office. The team helps consumers manage symptoms of the illness; they provide practical on-site support in coping with life's day-to-day demands. With the team approach, even with staff turnover, support can be consistently provided over time. The consumer is a client of the team, not of an individual staff member. Treatment, rehabilitation, and community support services are each tailored to the individual's needs. PACT provides up-to-date medication, and staff help people manage their medications, gain employment, and learn how to socialize and carry out a variety of tasks to live in regular housing alone or with a roommate. When a consumer can't do something on his or her own, the team steps in to help. Staff members help consumers get financial entitlements, housing, and non-psychiatric medical care. They oversee all medical care, including primary care and family planning. The team is consistently there for the consumer and family members, and the "one stop shopping" provided a cover for all aspects of community living.

NAMI members need to understand that

much of the strength and greater effectiveness of assertive community treatment comes from this approach. The team's direct, integrated provision of services brings medical/psychiatric treatment, rehabilitation, and community support services to severely ill consumers who otherwise would receive little or no care unless they were in a crisis that the community could not disregard. The team also deals with legal issues. When a consumer is arrested for minor offenses, the team intervenes. When a consumer is in jail, the team continues to see him or her, which often facilitates an earlier release.

The one-stop approach is especially effective in three areas: vocational services, alcohol and drug treatment, and helping consumers—usually women—develop skills as parents. We encourage and try to help consumers live in their own housing, if possible. This level of independence may take some time to accomplish, but having housing separate from parents (while remaining well supported by the PACT team) can make it easier for the consumer to relate to his or her family as an adult. Whatever happens, the team will be there supporting the consumer and family.

Chapter 19:

The Positive Future for Bipolar Disorder

Q...Dr. Fred, you have expressed some very positive ways that treatment and management can provide success for the bipolar at the present time. All things being equal, do you think that the future, for the bipolar, will provide an increased positive scientific outlook and that genotyping patients with bipolar disorder may be the answer for improved medication treatment?

A...There are so many ongoing scientific studies and research in the challenging area of mental illness, and bipolar disorder in particular, that all mental health care professionals and patients need to be positively aware of the changes that are now occurring. In order for the present bipolar to fully understand these futuristic changes, it is imperative that they stay positive about their own treatment and management. That means a positive continued goal toward achieving stability. It is a positive challenge for the bipolar to build a high level of understanding of who they are as a person, their self-esteem, self-confidence and self-knowledge. When that is accomplished, the future bipolar will welcome those new changes and move forward in new and positive ways in achieving a functional cure.

When the bipolar is ready to handle the fact that they need medical and therapeutic treatment, is when they can rightly blame the illness and not themselves. Certainly, that's easier said than done. When a bipolar is in attack mode, we naturally tend to see that person as the attacker. It's tough to view him/her as merely the instrument of the real, unseen force. We need to stay positive and look beyond the surface reality we're dealing with to see that it's the bipolar talking, the bipolar acting out. When we can see the illness as the underlying problem, we can start doing two things to turn the situation around:

-Stop making it worse. Blaming the person instead of the illness leads to confrontation which only worsens the situation. Stop pouring emotional fuel on a fire that's already blazing. When we blame the illness, we take some of the negative emotion out of the equation.

-Start making it better. When we recognize that bipolar disorder is an illness, we immediately know the solution: medical intervention. Obtaining that intervention when the disorder resists it, and finding effective medications that have tolerable . side effects, are often very difficult challenges, but at least we know what we're up against.

With this positive foundation of how a bipolar needs to look at their disorder and themselves, we can move ahead with the genomics of bipolar disorder and a very positive study for the bipolar.

By genotyping patients with bipolar disorder and using state-of-the-art imaging technology to evaluate drug effects, Mayo Clinic psychiatry researchers are learning more about the genetics of the disorder and how to better treat it.

Getting a handle on bipolar disorder is like riding a roller coaster with both patients and physicians — all hollering for stability. There is no diagnostic test to confirm bipolar disorder, and choosing the optimal drug therapy is a frustrating odyssey of trial and error. Manic episodes of overly excited states can quickly slide into states of deep depression. And some antidepressants, while effective in one individual, can trigger new rounds of uncontrollable mania in another.

Mark Frye, M.D. combines basic and clinical research with psychiatric practice in his new role as department chair of psychiatry and psychology at the Mayo Clinic. He is investigating ways to end the roller coaster ride, or at least to eliminate some of its rushes and surges. Dr. Frye, is using genotyping and brain scans in research to hopefully one day match the genetic profile of newly diagnosed patients with the most effective and least harmful drug to treat bipolar disorder.

Mayo Clinic is participating in an effort to rewrite accepted diagnostic criteria for bipolar disorder. "Diagnosis is currently made by confirming a set of signs and symptoms," says Dr. Frye. "It would be valuable as a clinician, when someone walks into our Mood Clinic here at Mayo, to have additional tools to help confirm diagnosis and guide treatment selection."

Nearly 14 million Americans (4.5 percent) experience some form of bipolar disorder, according to the National Institutes of Mental Health. It is linked to premature death and is a leading cause of disability for people ages 15 to 44.

Dr. Frye and colleagues are performing extensive blood tests, molecular testing and brain scans of patients with bipolar disorder to build the Mayo Clinic Individualized Medicine Biobank for Bipolar Disorder. The biological and clinical data collected in the biobank is intended as a resource for the bipolar research community to facilitate research leading to more accurate diagnosis, individualized drug therapies and increased knowledge about risk factors.

The biobank is a collaborative effort with the University of Minnesota, the Lindner Center of Hope in Cincinnati, Ohio, and all Mayo Clinic campuses. The goal is to include data from 2,000 individuals between the ages of 18 and 80. Genetic samples are usually collected by Mayo's Clinical Research Unit and stored in the Biospecimens Accessioning and Processing (BAP) Shared Resource core facility.

Accessioning and processing of specimens is the first step in the biobank archiving process. "Our hope is that biobank data may one day help identify the right treatment for the right patient," says Dr. Frye. "A good example of this is when clinicians struggle as whether or not to use antidepressants in the depressive phase of bipolar disorder. While not a common event, some patients can develop an antidepressant-induced mania. Right now, we're looking at the most commonly prescribed antidepressants, SSRIs like Prozac, Paxil and Zoloft."

Dr. Frye says the biobank can be used in different ways. In the case of antidepressant-induced mania, they are looking for patients who became manic while on Prozac and compare them with patients who were on the drug for the same time and did not become manic. This is called a case-control design. Using someone who had never been on Prozac as a control would be a bad comparison.

The team is also looking for genes that confer risk of developing bipolar disorder. In these double blind studies, the control group will come from the 20,000 participants in the Mayo Clinic Biobank. The scientists who conduct the lab analysis will be "blind" to the patients' diagnosis.

"Our research work is looking at whether a set of genes associated with this adverse outcome can be identified in such a way that future patients, when depressed, can be given alternative medications or psychotherapy."

In a clinical case conference (NEJM 2011), Dr. Frye reviewed a comprehensive analysis of 15 trials comparing short-term treatment with common antidepressant drugs that had no major benefit.

There are brain regions that implicated bipolar disorder, specifically the anterior cingulate. "There is great need to better understand the neurobiology of bipolar depression and develop novel treatments. Some of our earlier work had characterized bipolar depression as having an increase in glutamate in the anterior cingulate, which is a brain region, implicated or associated with depression. Furthermore, we saw a change in glutamine that was linked to clinical remission of depressive symptoms in the presence of lamotrigine." This, he thought, warranted further investigation.

Dr. Frye is now recruiting for a five-year clinical trial to evaluate the effectiveness of lamotrigine treatment for bipolar disorder. Lamotrigine is an anticonvulsive drug that appears to improve mood stability. The trial, funded by the National Institutes of Health (NIH), studies glutamate and glutamine concentrations in brain regions implicated in bipolar disorder to evaluate their effect on clinical remission.

Participants undergo brain imaging with proton magnetic resonance spectroscopy before and after 12 weeks of treatment with Lamotrigine. The imaging technology is a non-invasive method of evaluating the biochemical mechanism of drug action.

David Mrazek, M.D., has done extensive research on how best to individualize psychiatric medications. Dr. Mrazek has long been interested in pharmacogenomics, the science of discovering the genetic basis for individual variations in drug response. He was instrumental in developing a DNA test that can reveal whether a patient has one or more genes that interfere with the body's metabolism of commonly prescribed antidepressant drugs.

Dr. Mrazek notes that treatments can vary drastically even for the same diagnosis within the same family. In his book, Psychiatric Pharmacogenomics, he cites a case study in which both parents and their twin sons were diagnosed with depression. Surprisingly, each reacted differently to the same drug. Subsequent genotyping revealed different enzymatic activity levels that influenced whether the drug stimulated normal, slow or rapid metabolizing of the drug. "The ultimate goal is determining how to prescribe the right drug for the right patients at the right dose," Dr. Mrazek says.

Dr. Frye's medical career was initially directed toward internal medicine. Since transitioning to psychiatry, he has narrowed his focus to bipolar disorder, including a fellowship at the National Institute of Mental Health (NIMH) at the NIH and eight years directing UCLA's Bipolar Disorder Research Program. "It was interacting with patients with mood disorders, in particular bipolar disorder, that led me into psychiatry," he says. "I got very engaged when I realized how much there was to discover through brain imaging, genomics and clinical trials. It's exciting to contemplate how research will enable us to better understand bipolar disorder so that we can develop more-effective therapies and achieve better quality outcomes for our patients."

Dr. Frye has a particular interest in early-onset bipolar disorder and the impact of delayed treatment in young people. In a collaborative study, he and other researchers found that half of 529 patients (mean age of 42) had their first symptoms before age 13 or in their adolescence years (JClinPsy 2010). "Our study, with lead author Robert M. Post, M.D. (of George Washington University), showed that individuals who have onset of the illness in adolescence versus in adult life tend to have a more difficult course," Dr. Frye says. "Is this biologically or genetically based or associated with psychosocial stress? We don't know the answers, but we do know they are less likely to respond to medications. We should be vigilant to correctly diagnose young people and identify the best.

Drug therapy for bipolar disorder has come a long way since its beginning, in 1970, when Lithium was approved. A second drug, Divalproex, or Depakote, an anticonvulsant, became available in 1994. Today, drugs approved for bipolar treatment include mood stabilizers, anticonvulsants and antipsychotics. However, each comes with side effects ranging from mildly inconvenient to serious, rare, side effects. While there is need to develop new effective treatments that have less side effect burden, there is a greater need to individualize the treatment of bipolar disorder by finding the right medication for the right patient at the right time. Dr. Frye is confident that the Individualized Medicine Biobank for Bipolar Disorder will do much to move the field along.

Another very positive research is a study that discusses the Gene Abnormalities in Bipolar Disorder. Although it is not yet known if or how the suspect genetic variation might affect the balance machinery, the results point to the possibility that bipolar disorder might stem, at least in part, from the malfunction of ion channels.

Sklar, Shaun Purcell, Ph.D., and Nick Craddock, M.D., Ph.D., along with a large group of international collaborators, report on their findings online in Nature Genetics.

"Faced with little agreement among previous studies searching for the genomic hot spots in bipolar disorder, these researchers pooled their data for maximal statistical power and unearthed surprising results," said NIMH Director Thomas R. Insel, M.D. "Improved understanding of these abnormalities could lead to new hope for the millions of Americans affected by bipolar disorder."

In the first such genome-wide association study for bipolar disorder, NIMH researchers reported the strongest signal associated with bipolar in a gene that makes an enzyme involved with the action of Lithium. However, other chromosomal locations were most strongly associated with the disorder in two subsequent studies.

Since bipolar disorder is thought to involve many different gene variants, each exerting relatively small effects, researchers need large samples to detect relatively weak signals of bipolar association.

To boost their odds, Sklar and colleagues pooled data from the latter two previously published studies and one new study of their own. They also added additional samples from the STEP-BD study of Scottish and Irish families, and controls from the NIMH Genetics Repository. After examining about 1.8 million sites of genetic variation in 10,596 people – including 4,387 with bipolar disorder – the researchers found the two genes showing the strongest association among 14 disorder-associated chromosomal regions.

Variation in a gene called Ankyrin 3 (ANK3) showed the strongest association with bipolar disorder. The ANK3 protein is strategically located in the first part of neuronal extensions called axons and is part of the cellular machinery that decides whether a neuron will fire. Co-authors of the paper had shown that in mouse brains, Lithium, the most common medication for preventing bipolar disorder episodes, reduces expression of ANK3.

Variation in a calcium channel gene found in the brain showed the second strongest association with bipolar disorder. This CACNA1C protein similarly regulates the influx and outflow of calcium, and is the site of interaction for a hypertension medication that has also been used in the treatment of bipolar disorder.

These findings are extremely positive in that the variation in a gene called Ankyrin 3 (ANK3) revealed the strongest association with bipolar disorder. The future with this type of research will continue to be the basis of continued long term bipolar stability and a functional cure.

One of the most important and most positive recent studies is the genetic risk of suicide in bipolar disorder, Virginia L. Willour, PhD, the leader of the study at John Hopkins' University, says they have identified a gene variant that makes people with bipolar disorder more likely to attempt suicide. The scientists looked at DNA from about 2,700 people with bipolar disorder where about half had attempted suicide and half had not. They found that the people whose DNA had a particular gene variant were from 1.4 to 3 times as likely to have attempted suicide, depending on how many copies of the variant were present. Studying additional DNA from over 3,000 more people with bipolar disorder confirmed these findings.

This particular gene "is thought to influence the same biological pathway as Lithium, a medication known to reduce the rate of suicidal behavior." Virginia L. Willour, PhD said, "What's promising are the implications of this work for learning more about the biology of suicide and the medications used to treat patients who may be at risk. Not everyone with bipolar disorder can take Lithium because of its side effects. If we could give them another option, well that would be fantastic."

Since the rate of suicide and attempted suicide is far higher among people with bipolar disorder than for the general public, research like this could be crucial for saving lives. Willour says more such studies, with larger samples, are needed, but that the results are very promising. Again I point out that Lithium seems to have a positive significant relationship between new genetic research and the neurotransmitters occurring in the brain's biochemistry.

It may be possible to predict bipolar mood swings. A very positive study indicates that patients who felt they could manage their moods did better than their peers. The study suggests that it is possible to predict future mood swings in bipolar people by monitoring their thoughts and behavior. In the new study, researchers from the Universities of Manchester and Lancaster in the United Kingdom followed 50 bipolar patients for a month, studying how they think and act.

Individuals who believed extreme things about their moods, for example, that their moods were completely out of their own control or that they had to keep active all the time to prevent becoming a failure, developed more mood problems in a month's time," study lead author Warren Mansell, of the University of Manchester's School of Psychological Sciences, said in a university news release.

"In contrast, people with bipolar disorder, who could let their moods pass as a normal reaction to stress or knew that they could manage their mood fared, well a month later," he added. "These findings are encouraging for talk therapies, such as CBT [cognitive behavioral therapy], that aim to help patients talk about their moods and change their thinking about them," Mansell said.

One of the most important subjects that I have been addressing is the ability for the bipolar to positively confront their levels of stress. A newly published study says that having a bipolar parent increases the everyday level of a key stress hormone. In fact the study results are more interesting than that. For one thing, they weren't looking at young children, but at offspring between the ages of 14 and 28, so many of the study participants were not actually living with the bipolar parent anymore - yet the stress effect continued.

"Previous research has shown that children of parents with bipolar disorder are four times as likely to develop mood disorders as those from parents without the condition," said the senior author Dr. Mark Ellenbogen. "The goal of our study was to determine how this is happening."

Researchers already knew that high levels of the stress hormone cortisol often occur in people who later develop bipolar disorder, and that high stress levels can contribute to developing bipolar. What is inherent in this study is that people with a bipolar parent react to both low-level and high-level stress by producing more cortisol than those with the same stress level but no bipolar parent.

Here's an illustration: Megan, age 22, has a parent with bipolar disorder. Her best friend Laura, also 22, does not. One day the two of them have a terrible fight and their stress levels go sky-high. But Megan's body produces a lot more cortisol than Laura's. No matter how much stress there is on a given day, any stress will consistently produce more cortisol in Megan than in Laura. Because both high cortisol levels and high stress can contribute to the development of bipolar disorder, Megan's risk of becoming bipolar is higher than Laura's. We know children of parents with bipolar are more likely to get bipolar themselves. But the point is, we now have a biological mechanism that could be part of the reason they're more likely to develop bipolar disorder. These results, said Dr. Ellenbogen, might lead to finding ways to prevent the increased sensitivity from developing.

His conclusion suggests that if Megan had learned better ways to cope with stress early in life, it could make it less likely that she'd go on to develop bipolar disorder. Again, I can't emphasize the importance of how Lithium plays such a significant role with brain research. Another positive study reveals that Lithium increases certain brain regions in bipolar disorder. This study was reviewed by John M.Grohol, Psy.D.

International research has significantly boosted scientists' understanding of brain structure differences in those with bipolar disorder, as well as how Lithium (introduced in 1971 and still considered one of the most effective treatments), affects brain anatomy.

Eleven international research groups collaborated in an immense research effort published in Biological Psychiatry, to gather brain images of adults with bipolar disorder. This mega-analysis allowed them to compare the brain structure differences between individuals with bipolar disorder and healthy subjects.

These studies identified differences, mostly reductions, in the size of brain regions associated with mood regulation in bipolar patients. These studies also provided evidence that certain treatments for bipolar disorder would increase the mass of these brain regions.

The brain images revealed that individuals suffering from bipolar disorder had increased right lateral ventricular, left temporal lobe, and right putamen volumes. Bipolar patients who were not taking Lithium had a reduction in cerebral and hippocampus volumes compared with the healthy subjects. However, individuals with bipolar disorder taking Lithium showed significantly increased hippocampus and amygdale volume compared with patients not treated with Lithium and healthy comparison subjects. A reduction in cerebral volume was also strongly associated with illness duration in bipolar individuals.

"This important mega-analysis provides strong support for regional brain structural alterations associated with bipolar disorder, but also sends a signal of hope those treatments for this disorder may reduce some of these deficits," commented Dr. John Krystal, editor of Biological Psychiatry.

Candida Fink, MD reported in a recent study entitled "Postural Control in Bipolar Disorder: Increased Sway Area and Decreased Dynamical Complexity," that Indiana University researchers measured and compared the magnitude of postural sway between study participants with and without bipolar disorder. The study involved 32 participants, 16 of whom carried the bipolar diagnosis. The control group was made up of 16 age-matched non-psychiatric healthy participants.

Participants were asked to stand as still as possible on a force platform for two minutes under four conditions: (1) eyes open-open base (feet apart); (2) eyes closed-open base; (3) eyes open-closed base (feet together); and (4) eyes closed-closed base.

The researchers postulated that because many of the structural, neurochemical, and functional abnormalities identified in the brains of those with bipolar disorder are also implicated in postural control, people with bipolar disorder would have less postural control and hence a greater magnitude of sway than those without a brain disorder. In other words, there's a connection between motor and mood disorders. The results supported their hypothesis.

The bipolar disorder group had increased sway area (diminished postural control), especially with the loss of visual information (eyes closed). The bipolar disorder group exhibited a loss of complexity – in this case, a diminished ability to make faster, small-scale postural adjustments. A major complication inherent in the study, as the researchers themselves point out, is that other factors may have influenced the diminished postural control of the participants with bipolar disorder – primarily medication.

"The approach we have chosen for this study, i.e., studying euthymic, medicated patients, clearly presents difficulties in the interpretation of the present results because it is difficult to determine what proportion of the effect size arises from underlying mechanisms associated with bipolar disorder and what effects were due to medications."

While neuroleptics tend to have a negative effect on sway dynamics, SSRIs and Lithium tend to have a positive effect. Another complication consists of variations in the course of illness among the bipolar group and a history of alcohol abuse for some participants. However, even when the researchers accounted for such variations, the results indicated a connection between mood and motor disorders consistent with that of other studies. This suggests that motor disorders may be a core component of bipolar disorder.

The findings here add another layer to the complex neurologic story of bipolar disorder. We have known for a long time that some movement disorders (i.e. Parkinson's and Huntington's) have high rates of mood symptoms. This research is working in the other direction – looking at motor symptoms in mood disorder.

While this research does not have immediate or obvious clinical use, it is valuable in evolving our understanding of bipolar disorder as a brain based condition with a variety of associated brain changes. If people with bipolar disorder feel like they are clumsy or uncoordinated, it may be helpful for them to hear that this is likely part of their mood disorder, rather than something they are doing wrong. Perhaps motor based interventions, including exercise or physical therapy, may become more important in the treatment of bipolar disorder or at least in improving quality of life with bipolar.

Another clinical use that I can think of is that we may eventually use movement symptoms as one piece of data in looking at high risk children, such as those born to people with bipolar disorder, and helping to tease out who among them has higher risk of actually developing the disorder.

The research of gender differences in bipolar disorder is somewhat limited.

However, I have gathered some important statics and made comparisons between men and women. Bipolar disorder develops in men and women in about equal numbers, but there are gender differences in the ways that the disorder manifests itself. There are several gender differences that differentiate diagnosis and treatment of bipolar disorder for men vs. women.

Women with bipolar disorder tend to report more episodes of depression than men. Women also experience more 'mixed' episodes (an episode which has simultaneous features of both mania and depression). Women are almost three times more likely than men to have a comorbid diagnosis (one or more diseases/ disorders or conditions that occur together with the primary condition). Two of the most common comorbid disorders for women with bipolar were alcoholism and anxiety disorder.

Women are more likely to have rapid-cycles (experience four or more episodes per year) than men. Proposed explanations for this include: effects of gonadal steroids (estrogen or testosterone), hypothyroidism (more common in women), and greater use of antidepressant medication in women, which has been reported to cause episodes of mania in people with bipolar disorder.

Thyroid imbalances are more common in women than in men. Other associated medical conditions that are seen more often in bipolar women than in men include migraines, obesity, anxiety and panic disorders.

Men, bipolar disorder typically begins earlier and is more severe than in women. Manic episodes tend to be particularly pronounced. In addition, men are more apt to act out during mania. Guys are more likely to be out drinking, fighting, and yelling at people on the street, which often lands them in jail or causes them to be hospitalized for mania. Men with bipolar disorder are also more likely than women to have problems with drug or alcohol abuse. Men are less likely than women to voluntarily seek medical care for psychological conditions, including bipolar disorder. Bipolar men are more at risk for suicide than women, because suicide is more common in males. Men are more likely to experience a manic episode first, while women are more likely to experience depression first.

Knowing the differences between men and women with bipolar disorder, we can begin to explore more positive treatments dealing with symptoms and management. One such direction is improvement of bipolar disorder with routine sleep patterns. I feel this information is vital to understanding connection between sleep patterns, the circadian rhythm, regular social rhythm, daily routines and bipolar disorder. Researchers say that sleep is connected to bipolar disorder. That is, past research has shown that bipolar patients have difficulty with sleep and often suffer from sleep-related problems. Now new research is showing that routine sleep schedules can actually be beneficial to the outcomes of bipolar disorder.

A new study which appears in the journal of the American College of Neuro Psychopharmacology (ANCP), examined two groups of adult bipolar patients receiving different treatment therapies. The study found that the group of patients who participated in interpersonal and rhythm therapies (these therapies involved the patients monitoring their daily routines) had longer periods without mania and depression. Researchers have believed for some time that bipolar disorder is greatly affected by the circadian rhythm or the body's internal clock, and these new findings only further support this idea.

It seems that sufferers of bipolar disorder tend to have more sensitive circadian systems than do others. As a result, a change in routine or sleep schedule can throw the internal clocks of bipolar sufferers off (more so than with the healthy population), and result in more frequent manic and depressive episodes for bipolar patients.

Ellen Frank, Ph.D., who conducted the new study at the University of Pittsburgh, School of Medicine had this to say about the findings: "Having already found that disruption in daily routines can make individuals with bipolar disorder vulnerable to new episodes of the disorder, we have now learned that working with patients to achieve and maintain regular social rhythms -- including regular sleep patterns and adequate physical activity -- will help to protect them against episodes of mania or depression."

The bipolar is always challenged with a need to work toward some semblance of long term positive stability. However, risks of relapse are always a possibility. Positive solution and control of maintaining stability needs constant consideration.

"There may be changes in the cellular level that cause cycling but their cause is unknown," says Joseph R. Calabrese, MD, director of the Mood Disorders Program at the Case Western Reserve University School of Medicine in Cleveland, Ohio. While the neurological causes of relapse are unknown, a few things are certain: those who are diagnosed with bipolar II are more likely to relapse than those with bipolar I. Their episodes of depression, mania or hypomania are often shorter than the episodes experienced by those with bipolar I but tend to return more often, according to Dr.Calabrese. It's also far more common to relapse into depression than into mania or hypomania. Dr.Calabrese estimates that in bipolar II, there is a 40-to-1 ratio of depression to mania; the ratio of depression to mania drops to 3-to-1 in bipolar I.

"The key to recovery is a low tolerance for relapse," says Dr.Calabrese. In fact, Roger S. McIntyre, MD, associate professor of psychiatry and pharmacology at the University of

Toronto and head of the Mood Disorders Psychopharmacology Unit at the University Health Network, believes that even the mildest symptoms of depression and mania should be treated as potentially hazardous. "The takeaway message is that we need to seek complete elimination of symptoms as our treatment objective!" he says.

As I finish this last Chapter, it is fitting to review the conditions and causes of bipolar disorder. I have maintained throughout this book that all of us with bipolar need simply keep a positive attitude along with the gained knowledge that I have presented here in this book. Part of this knowledge is a simple positive understanding of a neurotransmitter. So let's look deeply in to our brain and discover the five major neurotransmitters for bipolar disorder.

First, one must understand what neurons are. Neurons are cells that carry information through the brain and the body. They are the telephone and the world wide web of the bodily functions of human beings. Signals travel from neuron to neuron by crossing a tiny space called a synapse, which is a gap between two neurons. Neurotransmitters are used to cross this synapse. The first neuron sends these chemical signals to the second neuron, which has receptor sites to receive them. If the brain and body are not producing active amounts of neurotransmitters, then chemical signals get screwed up and the mind cannot be regulated properly. When drug companies offer their theory of a chemical imbalance, this notion is heavily oversimplified, and these common neurotransmitters are only five of hundreds that could affect bipolar disorder. Here are five of the most common neurotransmitters:

-Dopamine
Dopamine is the feel good neurotransmitter, controlling attention and focus. If levels of this amino acid are out of whack, someone with bipolar disorder will feel too good or overly sad.

-Glutamate
Glutamate is found in a number of processed foods including canned soups. This neurotransmitter is thought to charge the central nervous system, causing mania.

-GABA
Gaba amino butyric acid can cause mania or depression depending on the effects of other neurotransmitters.

-Neuropinephrine
Neuropinephrine is a form of adrenaline that regulates the fight or flight response in humans. Its function is to regulate anxiety and mood.

-Serotonin
This neurotransmitter has the effect of a sedative, controlling anxiety and fear. Serotonin is most commonly fingered as a cause in bipolar disorder, as this amino acid regulates so many different functions of the mind and body.

And now I would like to attempt a very difficult task. It requires my constant positive mind set that bipolar can be dealt with if we have full understanding of all the possible causes.

Bipolar disorder has been determined to affect the brain and behavior. The cause of bipolar disorder is a bit of a mystery. It is thought, however, to be triggered by a combination of events that include genetics, the environment, including stress or the way one is raised, and changes in the brain.

One of the possible causes of bipolar disorder is altered levels of neurotransmitters. Neurotransmitters, like serotonin and norepinephrine, may be the culprits of bipolar disorder, as these chemicals are associated with different moods. Imbalances of certain neurotransmitters in the brain can cause the extreme mood changes. Also, environmental factors or hormonal changes may trigger this imbalance.

Another potential cause of bipolar disorder is an altered brain structure. Images taken of the brains of people with bipolar disorder are often structurally different than the brains of healthy individuals. These changes in the brain's structure may begin to develop as early as in childhood, given that similar genetic factors are associated with bipolar disorder. Brain structure alone may not be the cause of bipolar disorder, but it can predispose a person to bipolar disorder.

The ups and downs of bipolar disorder also affect the brain differently. Brain images disclose that during periods of depression, the prefrontal cortex was shown to function abnormally. This was a dramatic change from the images of the brains of people in the manic phase of bipolar disorder, which showed an abnormally high metabolism throughout the whole brain.

Over time, bipolar disorder may permanently affect the brain. While this has not been studied to a great extent, the Society of Biological Psychiatry noted gradual differences in brain structures as people with bipolar disorder age. These studies, of course, would be of extreme interest to me. Now at the age of 70, I am continuously researching the effects of bipolar disorder on age and brain structure.

What is my personal conclusion about age and bipolar? Why have I been successful with maintaining over 28 years of episode free emotional stability? Perhaps, the answer lies within the contents of what you have just read in this book: The Power of Positivity!

THE END

Bibliography for *The Power of Positivity* by Fred L. Von Gunten, O.D.

-1. www.bphope.com-. Issue.aspxe-Winter-2007-Volume 3 Number1 bp/Magazine-Five Generations Understanding the Past-Building the Future. By Donna Jakel.

-2. Alloy LB, Abramson LY, Urosevic S, Walshaw PD, Nusslock R, Neeren AM, (December 2005). "The Psychosocial Context of Bipolar Disorder: Environmental, Cognitive, and Developmental Risk Factors". Clinical Psychology Review 25 (8): 1043–75. doi: .1016/j.cpr.2005.06.006. PMID http://www.ncbi.nlm.nih.gov/pubmed/16 140445.

-3. Gabriele S Leverich, Robert M Post, "Course of Bipolar Illness after History of Childhood Trauma". The Lancet, Volume 367, Issue 9516, Pages 1040–1042, April 1, 2006 doi:10.1016/S0140-6736(06)68450-XCite.

-4. Louisa D. Grandin, Lauren B. Alloy, Lyn Y. Abramson, "Childhood Stressful Life Events and Bipolar Spectrum Disorders". Journal of Social and Clinical

Psychology, 26 (4) pp460–478 doi: 10.1521/jscp.2007.26.4.460.

-5. Denisa Milucka, http://allabout-personalitydisorders.blogspot.com-.

-6. Page 89, The National Institute of Mental Health (NIMH), "Systematic Treatment Enhancement Program for Bipolar Disorder (STEP-BD)".

-7. NAMI, William Knoedler, M.D., directed and worked as the psychiatrist for the Program of Assertive Community Treatment (PACT) in Madison, Wisconsin from 1972-1997.

-8. The Genomics of Bipolar Disorder, Mark Frye, M.D., combines basic and clinical research with psychiatric practice in his new role as department chair, Mayo Clinic Psychiatry Research.

-9. Published: Sunday, August 17, 2008, 13:14 in Health & Medicine Source: NIH/ National Institute of Mental Health. Sklar, Shaun Purcell, Ph.D., also of MGH and the Stanley Center, and Nick Craddock, M.D., Ph.D., of Cardiff University.

-10. Virginia L. Willour, PhD, the leader of the study at John Hopkins' University.

"Genetic Risk of Suicide in Bipolar Disorder".

-11. Warren Mansell, of the University of Manchester's School of Psychological Sciences. "Prediction of Future Mood Swings in Bipolar People by Monitoring Their Thoughts and Behavior."

-12. C. S. Ostiguy, Ellenbogen M. A., Walker C. D., Walker E. F., Hodgins S. "Sensitivity to Stress Among the Offspring of Parents with Bipolar Disorder: a Study of Daytime Cortisol Levels." Psychological Medicine.

-13. John M.Grohol, Psy.D. and Dr. John Krystal, editor of Biological Psychiatry. "Lithium Increases Certain Brain Regions in Bipolar Disorder."

-14. Candida Fink, MD reported in a recent study entitled "Postural Control in Bipolar Disorder: Increased Sway Area and Decreased Dynamical Complexity," at Indiana University.

-15. Ellen Frank, Ph.D., University of Pittsburgh, School of Medicine. "Improvement of Bipolar Disorder with Routine Sleep Patterns."

-16, Joseph R. Calabrese, MD, director of

the Mood Disorders Program at the Case Western Reserve University School of Medicine in Cleveland, Ohio and Dr. Roger S. McIntyre, MD, associate professor of psychiatry and pharmacology at the University of Toronto and head of the Mood Disorders Psychopharmacology Unit at the University Health Network. "Bipolar Disorder and Dealing with Relapse."

About the Author

My name is Dr. Fred and I have been retired for over 13 years. I was an Optometrist, specializing in developmental and behavioral vision for more than 33 years. I am happily married to a lovely lady, 48 years and counting. She supported me during my bipolar episodes and I owe my life to her. At 70, I have knowledge and experience when it comes to dealing with Bipolar Disorder. My mission is to help others in achieving emotional stability without episodes. I've lived 50 years with Bipolar I. For the first 25 years, I dealt with over five episodes. Since then, I have transformed my life by changing my thoughts and committing to a consistent supply of Lithium. I've maintained years of "episode-free emotional stability." Some would classify this as a "Functional Bipolar." Perhaps I might classify it as "Functionally Cured." I was one of the first to receive Lithium when the FDA approved it in 1971. It has kept me stable for the last 27 years, along with knowing the "Power of Being Positive with Bipolar Disorder."

Linda and Fred Von Gunten

Made in the USA
Coppell, TX
21 March 2021